OPPOSING VIEWPOINTS® SERIES

Race Relations

Other Books of Related Interest:

Opposing Viewpoints Series

Ethics

Human Rights

Illegal Immigration

Social Justice

Urban America

The U.S. Latino Community

Current Controversies Series

Immigration

Racism

At Issue Series

Racial Profiling

Should the U.S. Be Multilingual?

Should the U.S. Close Its Borders?

What Rights Should Illegal Immigrants Have?

Women in Islam

"Congress shall make no law ... abridging the freedom of speech, or of the press."

First Amendment to the U.S. Constitution

The basic foundation of our democracy is the First Amendment guarantee of freedom of expression. The *Opposing Viewpoints* Series is dedicated to the concept of this basic freedom and the idea that it is more important to practice it than to enshrine it.

Race Relations

Karen Miller, Book Editor

GREENHAVEN PRESS
A part of Gale, Cengage Learning

Detroit • New York • San Francisco • New Haven, Conn • Waterville, Maine • London

GALE
CENGAGE Learning·

Christine Nasso, *Publisher*
Elizabeth Des Chenes, *Managing Editor*

© 2011 Greenhaven Press, a part of Gale, Cengage Learning

Gale and Greenhaven Press are registered trademarks used herein under license.

For more information, contact:
Greenhaven Press
27500 Drake Rd.
Farmington Hills, MI 48331-3535
Or you can visit our Internet site at gale.cengage.com

For product information and technology assistance, contact us at

Gale Customer Support, 1-800-877-4253
For permission to use material from this text or product, submit all requests online at www.cengage.com/permissions

Further permissions questions can be emailed to permissionrequest@cengage.com.

Articles in Greenhaven Press anthologies are often edited for length to meet page require-ments. In addition, original titles of these works are changed to clearly present the main thesis and to explicitly indicate the author's opinion. Every effort is made to ensure that Greenhaven Press accurately reflects the original intent of the authors. Every effort has been made to trace the owners of copyrighted material.

Cover image copyright © Colin Anderson/Blend Images/Getty Images.

LIBRARY OF CONGRESS CATALOGING-IN-PUBLICATION DATA

Race relations / Karen Miller, book editor.
    p. cm. -- (Opposing viewpoints)
    Includes bibliographical references and index.
    ISBN 978-0-7377-4986-1 (hardcover) -- ISBN 978-0-7377-4987-8 (pbk.)
    1. Race discrimination--Juvenile literature. 2. Race relations--Juvenile literature.
    3. Race relations--Government policy. I. Miller, Karen, 1973-
    HT1521.R337 2011
    305.800973--dc22
                                                                        2010028939

Printed in the United States of America
1 2 3 4 5 6 7 14 13 12 11 10

Contents

Why Consider Opposing Viewpoints?

> *"The only way in which a human being can make some approach to knowing the whole of a subject is by hearing what can be said about it by persons of every variety of opinion and studying all modes in which it can be looked at by every character of mind. No wise man ever acquired his wisdom in any mode but this."*
>
> John Stuart Mill

In our media-intensive culture it is not difficult to find differing opinions. Thousands of newspapers and magazines and dozens of radio and television talk shows resound with differing points of view. The difficulty lies in deciding which opinion to agree with and which "experts" seem the most credible. The more inundated we become with differing opinions and claims, the more essential it is to hone critical reading and thinking skills to evaluate these ideas. Opposing Viewpoints books address this problem directly by presenting stimulating debates that can be used to enhance and teach these skills. The varied opinions contained in each book examine many different aspects of a single issue. While examining these conveniently edited opposing views, readers can develop critical thinking skills such as the ability to compare and contrast authors' credibility, facts, argumentation styles, use of persuasive techniques, and other stylistic tools. In short, the Opposing Viewpoints Series is an ideal way to attain the higher-level thinking and reading skills so essential in a culture of diverse and contradictory opinions.

In addition to providing a tool for critical thinking, *Opposing Viewpoints* books challenge readers to question their own strongly held opinions and assumptions. Most people form their opinions on the basis of upbringing, peer pressure, and personal, cultural, or professional bias. By reading carefully balanced opposing views, readers must directly confront new ideas as well as the opinions of those with whom they disagree. This is not to argue simplistically that everyone who reads opposing views will—or should—change his or her opinion. Instead, the series enhances readers' understanding of their own views by encouraging confrontation with opposing ideas. Careful examination of others' views can lead to the readers' understanding of the logical inconsistencies in their own opinions, perspective on why they hold an opinion, and the consideration of the possibility that their opinion requires further evaluation.

Evaluating Other Opinions

To ensure that this type of examination occurs, *Opposing Viewpoints* books present all types of opinions. Prominent spokespeople on different sides of each issue as well as well-known professionals from many disciplines challenge the reader. An additional goal of the series is to provide a forum for other, less known, or even unpopular viewpoints. The opinion of an ordinary person who has had to make the decision to cut off life support from a terminally ill relative, for example, may be just as valuable and provide just as much insight as a medical ethicist's professional opinion. The editors have two additional purposes in including these less known views. One, the editors encourage readers to respect others' opinions—even when not enhanced by professional credibility. It is only by reading or listening to and objectively evaluating others' ideas that one can determine whether they are worthy of consideration. Two, the inclusion of such viewpoints encourages the important critical thinking skill of objectively evaluating an author's credentials and bias. This evaluation will illuminate an author's reasons for taking a particular stance on an issue and will aid in readers' evaluation of the author's ideas.

It is our hope that these books will give readers a deeper understanding of the issues debated and an appreciation of the complexity of even seemingly simple issues when good and honest people disagree. This awareness is particularly important in a democratic society such as ours in which people enter into public debate to determine the common good. Those with whom one disagrees should not be regarded as enemies but rather as people whose views deserve careful examination and may shed light on one's own.

Thomas Jefferson once said that "difference of opinion leads to inquiry, and inquiry to truth." Jefferson, a broadly educated man, argued that "if a nation expects to be ignorant and free . . . it expects what never was and never will be." As individuals and as a nation, it is imperative that we consider the opinions of others and examine them with skill and discernment. The *Opposing Viewpoints* Series is intended to help readers achieve this goal.

David L. Bender and Bruno Leone,
Founders

Introduction

"I miss the '70's where you had shows like The Jefferson's *and* All in the Family *where black people could be black and white people could be white. Racists could be racists, and non-racists could be non-racists, but it was talked about. You could form your own opinion as to how ignorant or how reasonable these people were being."*

—American singer
and actress Queen Latifah

On February 15, 2010, a group of students at the University of California in San Diego hosted a theme party called "The Compton Cookout." Invitations encouraged guests to wear chains and cheap clothes, and to speak loudly; they encouraged females to dress as "ghetto chicks" with "gold teeth," who would "start fights and drama, and wear cheap clothes." The party theme was based on stereotypes about the primarily African American population of Compton, a city in southern Los Angeles County once listed by the U.S. Federal Bureau of Investigation (FBI) as one of the top twenty most dangerous cities in the nation. News of the party triggered outrage among the student body, particularly the Black Student Union, which in turn inspired a video mocking the controversy by a campus satirical media outlet, *The Koala*. This video made use of a racial slur, criticized protestors, and made a connection between HIV and race, further upsetting students on campus. *Koala*'s funding was suspended by Associated Students President Utsav Gupta, although it was later reinstated. Students protesting the event claimed that they were first offended by the party theme and the invitation language, and then later by *Koala*'s suggestion that they were in the wrong to take offense. Supporters of the party claim that the theme was just for fun, and that the gangster stereotype is an American trope that has been mocked and caricatured in popular culture long before they planned this party. They insist no harm was intended or committed.

Controversies like this one are not rare, despite the fact that the current class of university students is the most racially and ethnically diverse in history. Intrigued by this apparent contradiction, Brendesha Tynes, a professor of educational psychology at the University of Illinois, has been documenting photographs of racial situations posted by teenagers and college students on social networking sites such as MySpace and Facebook in an effort to learn more about their attitudes toward diversity. Tynes showed study participants a group of pictures of students at racially themed parties dressing and acting according to popular cultural stereotypes and asked them to respond to those photographs as if they'd encountered them on a friend's social networking site online. Participants were also interviewed about their attitudes toward racial privilege, institutional discrimination, and other topics about race. Tynes found a correlation between a participant's level of tolerance for the racially insensitive photographs and his or her opinion about the role race plays in society. The more "color-blind" a participant was—the degree to which that participant espoused the belief that race is an irrelevant concept kept alive by isolated victims who keep making an issue of it—the less offended that participant was by the scenes in the pictures. Tynes believes that dialogue about racism is needed now more than ever, and that the belief that racism is obsolete is not sufficient to make it so. Despite Americans' claims, many of whom have been newly inspired by the nation's first black president—Barack Obama—to have moved past racism into a "post-racial" society that has rendered race effectively irrelevant, matters of race still cause problems.

Professor Tynes is not the only academic to make this connection. Tim Wise, author of the 2009 book *Between Barack and a Hard Place*, calls this phenomenon "Racism 2.0" or "enlightened exceptionalism." His argument is that because so many exceptional minorities have overcome racial barriers, the general view of the minorities who don't is that they have personal character flaws rendering them unwilling or unable to achieve the standards of success promoted by (white) mainstream society. In the preface to the book, he suggests that white people voted for a black president in part to demonstrate they are not racist anymore so the proverbial book on racism can be closed for once and for all. Wise's opinion is supported by the fact that the United States did not attend the World Conference Against Racism/Durban Review Conference held in Geneva, Switzerland, in April 2009 (it was not the only Western nation to skip it) even though racial tension, hate crimes, and mass movements of refugees permeate modern global society.

Racism 2.0 has not, however, completely consumed American society. Eric Holder, President Obama's attorney general and the first African American attorney general of the United States, lambasted American complacency about race relations in a speech to Department of Justice employees for Black History Month in February 2009. He accused the United States of being a "nation of cowards" and urged Americans to begin speaking honestly again about race and inequality, and its impact on their culture. *Opposing Viewpoints: Race Relations* attempts to examine these issues. Its four chapters—What Is the Basis of Race?, How Does Society Impact Race Relations?, How Does Government Affect Race Relations?, and What Does the Future Hold for Race Relations?—identify some of the topics about race relations that occupy national discourse, investigate the origins of these conflicts, and explore ways to improve relations in the future.

OPPOSING
VIEWPOINTS®
SERIES

CHAPTER 1

What Is the Basis of Race?

Chapter Preface

Science and race have had an uneasy relationship for a very long time. Compelled at first by the desire to just explain why people around the world looked and behaved so differently from each other, science often became a tool to justify why some groups of people ought to be treated differently, too. Craniologists in the 19th Century claimed that race could be determined by measuring the size and angle of a person's face; polygenists claimed that humans of different races evolved from separate lineages and thus were superior or inferior to the others. Even after Charles Darwin's theory of evolution convinced scientists that humans shared the same origin, social Darwinism and eugenics programs were implemented to remove "undesirable" humans from the breeding pool. Science and biology have been used to justify slavery, forced sterilization programs, the Holocaust of World War II, and countless other social crimes based on race and genetics. It is no wonder, then, that the announcement of a pharmaceutical drug that worked better for African Americans than white Americans was met with disbelief and some amount of outrage.

BiDil is the trade name of two drugs combined and produced by NitroMed that was approved by the Food and Drug Administration in 2005. It was officially labeled the first "ethnic" drug because it was approved specifically for African Americans, a group of people who generally do not respond well to conventional treatments for congestive heart failure but who responded well to this pill. Doctors were happy to have another tool to help patients; pharmaceutical companies were happy that a precedent of "ethnic" drugs had been set so they could start marketing and manufacturing new products. Other scientists, politicians, academics, and community leaders were not happy at all. Critics of the study establishing the drug's effectiveness for African Americans pointed out that the test subjects volunteered as self-identified African Americans rather than being identified as African Americans by an objective test—because there isn't one. African American and white American families have been mixing for hundreds of years and share a significant amount of genetic history. Politicians and academics objected on practical and theoretical grounds to the government approval of BiDil for African Americans only—thereby denying many people access to a drug because of their race. Community leaders, especially those old enough to personally remember the civil rights movements of the 20th Century, considered any government action based solely on race to be a dangerous step backward after decades of hard work to eliminate racism.

Complicating the issue is the fact that, despite there being no biological markers or genetic evidence for race, some diseases and disorders appear disproportionately in certain racial and ethnic groups: sickle-cell anemia in sub-Saharan Africans and their descendants, Tay-Sachs in Ashkenazi Jews and French Canadians, type 2 diabetes among the Pima Native Americans, and Ellis-van Creveld syndrome among the Amish in Pennsylvania. But a gene is not a race, and if Ellis-van Creveld is unusually prevalent among Amish people, it may be because Amish people tend to marry other Amish people and pass it along. People living in sub-Saharan Africa are far more likely to marry each other than someone from Europe. Family heritage overlaps with racial heritage, and both are influenced by culture and environment, and it can be very difficult to extract data that point to one factor or another.

For every reason to disregard race in medicine there is another reason to consider it. In the end, the best doctors work closely with their patients as individuals to identify the best solutions to their health problems, and consider race when it makes sense to. Society at large, however, will continue to argue over whether race can influence health and treatment, and if it is ethical or reasonable to do so. The following chapter examines some of the arguments for biological definitions and origins of race, and to what extent race is a social construction with no natural basis.

*"This kind of DNA testing ... can tell
you if you belong to a particular ethnic
group."*

DNA Testing Can Provide
Clues to Race and Ethnicity

Karen Goldberg Goff

Karen Goldberg Goff has been a reporter for the Washington
Times *since 1992. She writes feature-length stories on a variety
of topics, including family issues, pop culture, health, food, and
technology. The following article describes the resources available
to consumers who wish to have their DNA tested for genetic
markers common to certain racial and ethnic groups. Goff points
out, however, that the ancestor-search industry is still new and
unregulated, and that until the science is improved, results may
be confusing or vague.*

As you read, consider the following questions:

1. What, according to the author, did a paternal lineage
   test reveal about Thomas Jefferson?

2. What is the link, according to Goff, between genetic
   testing, ethnic groups, and disease?

Karen Goldberg Goff, "DNA Tests Help Genealogists Only So Far," *Washington Times*,
March 11, 2009. Copyright © 2009 The Washington Times, LLC. Reproduced by permission.

3. According to the author, what concerns does the American Society of Human Genetics have about commercial ancestry testing?

The path to researching one's family history often used to hit a wall where the paper trail ended. Since the advent of the Internet, though, genealogists have had a virtual world of information available to them without traveling the globe.

More recently, genetic testing has been made available to the masses to more definitively determine where your ancestors came from. A quick swab of a few cheek cells, and one can go back thousands of years, well before there were historical documents.

The process is not without caveats, however. Genetic tests sometimes leave testers more confused than when the process began, particularly in the black community, where records may only go back to the slave trade.

"Testing is only filling in a small segment of the big picture," says Troy Duster, a sociology professor at New York University [NYU]. "That's part of the problem. Some people feel that maybe knowing a little is better than not knowing anything, but it can provide people with a false sense of connection."

Mr. Duster points out that only some of the ancestors—as few as two of 64 great-great-great-great grandparents—can be identified with current DNA testing. Genetic DNA tests are quick to rule out whether someone belongs to a particular group, but they don't take into account the entire genetic makeup, Mr. Duster says. Testing only takes into account biology, and not affiliation with certain groups by way of language, culture or other customs, he says.

DNA Testing Goes Mainstream

Genetic DNA testing technology has been around nearly a decade but has gained popularity in the past 18 months as testing kits became increasingly more inexpensive and available.

More than a dozen companies now offer such services. Ancestry.com, part of the largest group of online genealogy resources, began offering DNA services in October 2007 and recently lowered the price of its 33-marker paternal lineage test from $149 to $79.

"You don't have to be a hard-core genealogist to get excited about what DNA can tell you," says Brett Folkman, Ancestry.com's vice president of DNA product. "DNA definitely has huge promise as a big breakthrough for genealogy. Stories may or may not be true. DNA can prove or disprove them."

Here's how it works: The most popular test is the paternal lineage, which analyzes DNA in the Y chromosome (passed virtually unchanged from father to son). Since this test analyzes paternal contributions, only men can take it. It was this type of testing that recently established that Thomas Jefferson probably had children with his slave, Sally Hemings.

Also available is the mitochondrial DNA test, which reveals a mother's line. This type of testing recently proved that remains found in Russia in the early 1990s were members of the Romanov royal family, killed in 1918.

Test participants in Ancestry.com's program, for instance, receive analysis of the ancient group to which their ancestors belonged, a map of the group's migration pattern, online results that can potentially identify genetic cousins, and access to a large database of potential relatives.

Family Tree DNA, a Houston company that has been offering DNA testing since 2000, has built up a database of more than 200,000 participants. Family Tree DNA tests start at $99. The company works in conjunction with National Geographic, whose Genographic Project has been mapping the migration pattern of humankind since 2005.

Max Blankfeld, vice president for marketing and operations for Family Tree DNA, says its database is not public, but participants sign a release if they want their records included in the database. Most do, because the more people in the database, the greater volume of information will be out there for historians to access.

"In the case of relevant matches, we provide name and e-mail information," Mr. Blankfeld says. "It is the ultimate social network."

Through DNA testing, Family Tree and other genealogy companies build surname projects. Family Tree has a listing of more than 5,200 surnames, which further aids genealogists in finding common ancestors and discovering new branches of their family tree.

Genealogical testing companies do not provide medical information, Mr. Folkman says. This kind of DNA testing will not tell you if you have the gene for a particular disease. However, it can tell you if you belong to a particular ethnic group—and sometimes certain ethnic groups have a propensity for a particular disease. Genealogical DNA also cannot personally identify someone in the same manner it would be used in a criminal investigation.

The Technology Is Evolving

As the number of people looking for connections has grown, so has the number of critics of DNA testing. The technology does not come without caveats.

Harvard [University] African American Studies professor Henry Louis Gates Jr. helped popularize DNA testing with a 2006 PBS special *African American Lives*, but after repeated tests with different companies, Mr. Gates said last year he had been given conflicting results. One company told him his maternal ancestors were Egyptian; another told him they were European.

Edward Ball, author of the book *The Genetic Strand*, writes that he had some ancestral hair samples tested. One company told him they were American Indian. Another company told him he had African genes but not American Indian genes. Still another told him his people came from Northern Europe.

Mr. Duster of NYU calls the business of genetic DNA testing "an unregulated no-man's land." He says he would like to see guidelines and transparency as the business evolves.

"Any company can claim that their laboratories can analyze your DNA to provide accurate information about your ancestry," Mr. Duster says. "But if three different companies provide three different answers [as a report on CBS' *60 Minutes* did in 2007], what is a consumer to do? Which company is correct? There is no way of knowing, since we have no 'gold standard' for excellence or professional self-policing."

The American Society of Human Genetics (ASHG) has similar concerns. The group says that those who undergo ancestry testing often do not realize the tests are probabilistic and can reach incorrect conclusions, causing emotional distress if test results are unexpected or undesired.

The ASHG says consumers frequently purchase these tests to learn about their race or ethnicity yet there is no clear-cut connection between an individual's DNA and racial affiliation.

ASHG President Aravinda Chakravarti, from Johns Hopkins University School of Medicine, says the group recommends greater efforts on the part of both industry and academia to make the limitations of ancestry-testing estimation more clear. Consumers, meanwhile, have a responsibility to avail themselves of information about ancestry testing and to strive to better understand the implications and limitations of these tests.

The society also called for additional research to understand testing's accuracy and for guidelines to be developed for ethical use of testing and research.

> "When individuals lie at the cusp of the white/nonwhite divide, we unconsciously categorize them as the Other when they engage in wrongdoing but blend them into the white when they behave within social norms."

Racial Categories Are Social Constructions

John Tehranian

John Tehranian is a law professor at Chapman University School of Law and the author of numerous works on race, civil rights, and constitutional law. The following viewpoint is excerpted from his book, Whitewashed, *a study of how Middle Eastern Americans are faced with increasing levels of discrimination but cannot readily find redress because they are legally classified as "white." Tehranian looks specifically at how "selective racialization"—emphasizing foreignness only when a person is undesirable—has affected how Middle Eastern and other ethnic Americans identify themselves publicly and privately, and also how inconsistently categories of race are defined.*

As you read, consider the following questions:

1. According to the author, what ethnicity is the singer Shakira most commonly associated with?

2. How, according to the author, does selective racialization in the Disney movie *Aladdin* solidify negative stereotypes about Arabic traits and behaviors?

3. What was Pete Hernandez challenging in the *Hernandez v. Texas* suit, according to Tehranian?

In society at large, Middle Easterners are consistently subjected to a process of *selective racialization*. This largely undocumented and predominantly subconscious mechanism has profound ramifications. Systematically, famous individuals of Middle Eastern descent are usually perceived as white. Meanwhile, *infamous* individuals of Middle Eastern descent are usually categorized as Middle Eastern. When Middle Eastern actors conform to social norms and advance positive values and conduct, their racial identity as the Other recedes to the background as they merge into the great white abyss. By contrast, when Middle Eastern actors engage in transgressive behavior, their racial identity as the Other immediately becomes a central, defining characteristic of who they are. The result is an endless feedback loop that calcifies popular prejudices. Wholesome and socially redeeming activities, which might otherwise subvert public misperceptions of the community, do not get associated with Middle Eastern identity. By contrast, the image of transgression is continually correlated with the Middle Eastern racial category, serving only to reinforce negative connotations with the community.

Our country is filled with individuals of Middle Eastern descent who have contributed constructively to American society. Yet surprisingly few of these Americans are actually perceived as Middle Easterners. Instead, their ethnicity is frequently whitewashed. On one hand, this fact highlights the assimilability of Middle Eastern immigrants in the United States. On the other hand, it creates a problematic signposting of Middle Eastern identity when it becomes associated with transgressive activities.

The long list of Middle Eastern Americans includes individuals from virtually every aspect of American life, including athletes such as tennis player Andre Agassi (Persian/Armenian), Indy 500 champion Bobby Rahal (Lebanese), and NFL quarterbacks Doug Flutie and Jeff George (both Lebanese); entertainers such as actresses Cher (Armenian), Kathy Najimi (Lebanese), Catherine Bell (half Persian), and Gabrielle Anwar (half Persian), actors Danny Thomas (Lebanese) and Tony Shalhoub (Lebanese), radio deejay Casey Kasem (Palestinian/ Lebanese), and singer Paul Anka (Lebanese); prominent entrepreneurs such as hoteliers the Maloof family (Lebanese) and Apple CEO Steve Jobs (half Syrian); and politicians and activists such as former New Hampshire governor and White House chief of staff John Sununu (Lebanese), former senator George Mitchell (half Lebanese), and prominent consumer advocate and presidential candidate Ralph Nader (Lebanese/Egyptian). Even "good" Middle Easterners who are perceived as nonwhite are not racialized as Middle Eastern. For example, although they are both half Lebanese, neither Salma Hayek, a famous actress, nor Shakira, an internationally renowned singer, is identified as Middle Eastern. Instead, they are almost universally considered Latina.

Race Is Inconsistently Identified

Some observers might point to the whitewashing of Americans of Middle Eastern descent as evidence of our evolving colorblindness. But such an argument is belied by the systematic racialization of transgressive individuals. When individuals lie at the cusp of the white/nonwhite divide, we unconsciously categorize them as the Other when they engage in wrongdoing but blend them into the white when they behave within social norms. Andre Agassi is a (white) tennis player, and Ralph Nader is a (white) politician. But Osama bin Laden is labeled an Arab terrorist and the Ayatollah Khomeini was a Middle Eastern Islamic fundamentalist. The act of selective racialization is by no means limited to geopolitical struggles. It occurs on a far more pedestrian, but nevertheless important, level. Take the case of Dodi Al-Fayed, the wealthy businessman who was dating [British] Princess Diana following her divorce from Prince Charles. The escapades of the two, rumored to be engaged at the time of their deaths, were the subject of extensive media coverage. Throughout their relationship, Al-Fayed was repeatedly portrayed as an *Arab* businessman and *Middle Eastern* playboy—not merely an Englishman or a businessman without reference to his face. In other words, he was racialized. And the reason is clear: he was engaging in transgressive behavior, stealing away with the People's princess.

Other examples abound. Recently, Zenadine Zidane, a member of the French national soccer team, viciously headbutted Italian player Marco Materazzi in the finals of the 2006 World Cup. Zidane's violent outburst likely cost his team the championship and has gone down as one of the most infamous incidents in soccer history. While the incident sullied Zidane's previously untarnished reputation, it also did something else: it racialized Zidane in the United States. In the aftermath of the incident, Zidane went from simply being an otherwise ordinary native-born (white) Frenchman on the Gallican national soccer team to becoming an Arab. American media reports highlighted his Algerian roots. The racial subtext was all too clear—there was an implicit association of his apparent predilection for violence with his Arab background. He had brazenly violated social norms with his headbutt and, as such, had become a transgressor. Simultaneously, he went from being white to becoming the Other.

The process of selective racialization occurs with regularity in the mass media, serving to bolster and legitimize existing stereotypes. Although all the characters in the Middle Eastern–themed Disney film *Aladdin* share Arab descent, they are only selectively racialized. The chief wrongdoers—the greedy bazaar merchants, the thief Kazim, and the main antagonist, Jafar—all possess exaggerated stereotypical features. Both Kazim and Jafar sport thick Arab accents, facial hair, and prominent hooked noses. By contrast, the movie's sympathetic protagonists—Aladdin, Princess Jasmine, and the Sultan—possess few of the features traditionally associated with Arabs. Instead, their physiognomy is quintessentially European, and they speak with no trace of a Middle Eastern accent. In other words, the transgressive characters are Arabized and the wholesome characters are Anglicized, thereby heightening negative stereotypes linked to Middle Easterners while concurrently reinforcing positive associations with whiteness. . . .

The phenomenon is not restricted to Middle Easterners, but can apply any time someone stands at the precipice of whiteness. In the world of baseball, Nomar Garciaparra, a former Boston Red Sox all-star, used to undergo a process of selective racialization with his hometown fans. Garciaparra, who is of Mexican descent, is often mistaken as Italian. Caught at the edge of the white divide, his racial affiliation remains contested and subject to unconscious public perceptions. Whenever he found himself in a particularly hot stretch of hitting, Bostonians would hail him mirthfully on the street, cheering him with the words "Hey, paesano," a greeting popular between Italian Americans. Only when he lived up to his billing as the team captain and perennial all-star was he perceived as an Italian. On the other hand, when he was mired in a prolonged slump, the public not only turned on him but also viewed him in different racial terms. All of a sudden, instead of being acknowledged as a paesano, he would be decried as a "stupid Mexican." Through the process of selective

Racial Color Lines Are Temporary

A black-nonblack divide is taking shape, in which Asians and Latinos are not only closer to whites than blacks are to whites, but also closer to whites than to blacks at this point in time. Hence, America's color line may have moved toward a new demarcation that places many blacks in a position of disadvantage similar to that resulting from the traditional black-white divide. In essence, rather than erasing racial boundaries, the country may simply be reinventing a color line that continues to separate blacks from other racial/ethnic groups.

While a black-nonblack divide may depict the color line at the moment, it is also possible that a black-white divide might re-emerge. Whiteness as a category has expanded over time to incorporate new immigrant groups in the past, and it appears to be stretching yet again. Based on patterns of multiracial identification, Asians and Latinos may be the next in line to be white, with multiracial Asian-whites and Latino-whites at the head of the queue.

Jennifer Lee and Frank Bean,
"Reinventing the Color Line," Social Forces, 2007.

racialization, white continues to be imbued with positive associations while the Other continues to endure negative connotations. . . .

Choosing Ethnic and Racial Identities

Take the example of a doctor I once knew. He was born and grew up in Iran. He had then received his medical training in Switzerland, after which he and his wife had ultimately immigrated to the United States. When people asked where he was from, he would apparently say "Switzerland." Throughout his community, people thought of him and his Iranian wife as European. And I suspect that is just how he wanted it.

What is particularly interesting about this example is that the doctor and his family never engaged in a wholesale rejection of their ethnicity or cultural heritage. Their sense of identity and projection of it were far more complex than that. In fact, the doctor was a dedicated student of classical Persian poetry and prose and hosted a weekly gathering of Iranian immigrants at his house to discuss, in their native tongue, works in the Persian canon. But to the outside world he was Swiss. And who could blame the family for performing this act of covering? There is little doubt that it is a lot easier to be Swiss and deal with the attendant images of temporal precision, chocolate, neutrality, and the Red Cross than to be perceived as Iranian, when people immediately associate your ethnic identity with a host of unpleasantries.

The imprecise relationship between ethnicity and nationality arises in a broader context and represents a particular difficulty in conducting affirmative-action programs. Latin America has witnessed several waves of migration from Europe. Some of these immigrants have subsequently relocated to the United States. However, they sometimes draw on their intermediate stop in Latin America as a basis for claiming "Hispanic" heritage on school and job applications. In one sense, their choice is entirely warranted. *Hispanic* is generally not characterized as a "race" at all. The University of California at Los Angeles exemplifies this idea in its definition of Hispanic/Latino as "[p]ersons of Latin American (e.g., Central American, South American, Cuban, Puerto Rican) culture or origin, regardless of race." In another sense, if identification of Hispanic heritage is used for affirmative-action purposes and is meant to offset both past and present discrimination, such a practice dilutes the means-ends fit of remedial programs.

Many Iranians or Arabs of Jewish background cover by rationally exploiting mainstream (mis)perceptions of "Jewishness" as both a religion and an ethnicity. For example, although the Jewish Iranian population is relatively large, especially in Los Angeles, the very existence of a Jewish Iranian population is a surprise to the many people who view Iran as an Islamic monolith. By identifying themselves to the world as Jewish, these Jewish Iranians tend to avoid any further questions about their ethnicity, as people assume their ethnicity is Jewish and that they therefore are white (i.e., Ashkenazi Jewish) and not Middle Eastern. A Jewish Iranian poet I once knew demonstrated her profound awareness of the way in which this popular misperception could be exploited for assimilatory purposes. Explaining the extent of her Persian pride, she pointed out that she had embraced her Iranian heritage despite the obvious covering tactics at her disposal. "Since I'm Jewish, I don't have to be Iranian," she remarked. "Yet I choose to be." . . .

Fluid Racial Boundaries Are Judicially Solidified

Mexican Americans provide an instructive example of the tension between individual and collective interests, and of short- and long-term consequences. Like Middle Easterners, Latinos have suffered a problematic dualistic ontology [theory of being] of racial identification and a craving for whiteness that, in prior eras, has frustrated the vindication of their civil rights. Mexican Americans have often sought refuge in covering activities. Rodolfo Acuña, for example, notes the tendency of the Mexican American community in Los Angeles to emphasize its Spanish (i.e., European and white) roots. As he argues, many Mexican Americans have internalized an "anything but Mexican" mindset, or colonial mentality, that fuels their desire for white recognition and leads them to emphasize their Spanish, Italian, or French ancestry.

In prior eras, this irrepressible claim to whiteness has actually undermined civil rights efforts. In the landmark suit *Hernandez v. Texas*, Pete Hernandez challenged the systematic exclusion of Mexican Americans from juries in Jackson County, Texas. In response, the State of Texas claimed, among other things, that there was no racial discrimination occurring since individuals of Mexican descent were not a separate class from whites. The Supreme Court ultimately sided with Hernandez, holding that Mexicans were a distinct race from whites for equal protection purposes and that the Equal Protection Clause applied to all forms of race discrimination, not just discrimination against blacks. Surprisingly though, Hernandez faced strong opposition to his position from within the Mexican American community. Gustavo Garcia, a civil rights litigator of the time, commented, "Caucasians were on the jury. Mexicans are Caucasian. So what's all the fussing about?" To Mexican Americans such as Garcia, the recognition of their whiteness trumped the vindication of their legal and political rights or the preservation of equal protection under the law. This . . . parallels the extant Middle Eastern hunger for judicial affirmations of whiteness, even when it inures to the group's long-term detriment.

In sum, like the Irish, Slavs, Italians, Greeks, and Mexicans before them, Middle Eastern immigrants have sought to secure their position in American society through the ultimate prize of white recognition. The struggle, however, has not been easy. Formal recognition of whiteness by state and federal governments belies a history of discrimination against Americans of Middle Eastern descent. The wide range of both passing and covering strategies adopted by Middle Easterners reflects the response to this discrimination. Combined with the process of selective racialization, it is a practice that has grown increasingly problematic. The rewards for effective covering are, in the short term, positive. But in the aggregate, the phenomena of covering and selective racialization have helped to perpetuate negative stereotypes about Middle Easterners while frustrating the development of an effective community response to issues of concern for Middle Eastern Americans.

> *"At no point in the study did the children exhibit the . . . color-blindness that many adults expect."*

Children Are Naturally Aware of Racial Differences

Po Bronson and Ashley Merryman

Po Bronson and Ashley Merryman are collaborators who have published articles on the science of parenting in New York *and* Time *magazines. They have won the magazine journalism award from the American Association for the Advancement of Science and the award for outstanding journalism from the Council on Contemporary Families. The following viewpoint is excerpted from their book,* NurtureShock, *an exploration of modern parenting strategies and the science of how children learn and develop. The authors argue that children are aware of racial differences as infants, and that explicitly addressing these differences increases their acceptance of racial diversity.*

As you read, consider the following questions:

1. According to the authors, what decades-old assumption about children's perceptions of race has recently been questioned by child development researchers?

2. How do the authors define *essentialism*, especially in the context of children forming opinions about groups of people?

3. What evidence in her study supports Dr. Phyllis Katz's claim that there is no point in children's lives when they are unaware of racial differences?

The election of President Barack Obama has marked the beginning of a new era in race relations in the United States—but it hasn't resolved the question as to what we should tell children about race. If anything, it's pushed that issue to the forefront. Many parents have explicitly pointed out Obama's brown skin to their young children, to reinforce the message that anyone can rise to become a leader, and anyone—regardless of skin color—can be a friend, be loved, and be admired.

But still others are thinking it's better to say nothing at all about the president's race or ethnicity—because saying something about it unavoidably teaches a child a racial construct. They worry that even a positive statement ("It's wonderful that a black person can be president") will still encourage the child to see divisions within society. For them, the better course is just to let a young child learn by the example; what kids see is what they'll think is normal. For their early formative years, at least, let the children know a time when skin color does not matter.

A 2007 study in the *Journal of Marriage and Family* found that out of 17,000 families with kindergartners, 45% said they'd never, or almost never, discussed race issues with their children. But that was for all ethnicities. Nonwhite parents are about three times more likely to discuss race than white parents; 75% of the latter never, or almost never, talk about race.

For decades, we assumed that children will only see race when society points it out to them. That approach was shared by much of the scientific community—the view was that race was a societal issue best left to sociologists and demographers to figure out. However, child development researchers have increasingly begun to question that presumption. They argue that children see racial differences as much as they see the difference between pink and blue—but we tell kids that "pink" means for girls and blue is for boys. "White" and "black" are mysteries we leave them to figure out on their own.

It takes remarkably little for children to develop in-group preferences once a difference has been recognized. [University of Texas researcher Rebecca] Bigler ran an experiment in three preschool classrooms, where four- and five-year-olds, were lined up and given T-shirts. Half the kids were given blue T-shirts, half red. The children wore the shirts for three weeks. During that time, the teachers never mentioned their colors and never again grouped the kids by shirt color. The teachers never referred to the "Blues" or the "Reds." Bigler wanted to see what would happen to the children naturally, once color groupings had been established.

The kids didn't segregate in their behavior. They played with each other freely at recess. But when asked which color team was better to belong to, or which team might win a race, they chose their own color. They liked the kids in their own group more and believed they were smarter than the other color. "The Reds never showed hatred for Blues," Bigler observed. "It was more like, 'Blues are fine, but not as good as us.'" When Reds were asked how many Reds were nice, they'd answer "All of us." Asked how many Blues were nice, they'd answer "Some." Some of the Blues were mean, and some were dumb—but not the Reds.

Bigler's experiment seems to show how children will use whatever you give them to create divisions—seeming to confirm that race becomes an issue only if we make it an issue. So why does Bigler think it's important to talk to children about race, as early as age three?

Her reasoning is that kids are *developmentally* prone to in-group favoritism; they're going to form these preferences on their own. Children categorize everything from food to toys to people at a young age. However, it takes years before their cognitive abilities allow them to successfully use more than one attribute to categorize anything. In the meantime, the attribute they rely on is that which is the most clearly visible.

Bigler contends that once a child identifies someone as most closely resembling himself, the child likes that person the most. And the child extends their shared appearances much further—believing that everything else he likes, those who look similar to him like as well. Anything he doesn't like thus belongs to those who look the least similar to him. The spontaneous tendency to assume your group shares characteristics—such as niceness, or smarts—is called *essentialism*. Kids never think groups are random.

We might imagine we're creating color-blind environments for children, but differences in skin color or hair or weight are like differences in gender—they're plainly visible. We don't have to label them for them to become salient. Even if no teacher or parent mentions race, kids will use skin color on their own, the same way they use T-shirt colors.

Within the past decade or so, developmental psychologists have begun a handful of longitudinal studies [involving observations over time] to determine exactly when children develop bias—the general premise being that the earlier the bias manifests itself, the more likely it is driven by developmental processes.

Dr. Phyllis Katz, then a professor at the University of Colorado, led one such study—following 100 black children and 100 white children for their first six years. She tested these children and their parents nine times during those six years, with the first test at six months old.

How do researchers test a six-month-old? It's actually a common test in child development research. They show babies photographs of faces, measuring how long the child's attention remains on the photographs. Looking at a photograph longer does not indicate a preference for that photo, or for that face. Rather, looking longer means the child's brain finds the face to be out of the ordinary; she stares at it longer because her brain is trying to make sense of it. So faces that are familiar actually get shorter visual attention. Children will stare significantly longer at photographs of faces that are a different race from their parents. Race itself has no ethnic meaning, per se—but children's brains are noticing skin color differences and trying to understand their meaning.

When the kids turned three, Katz showed them photographs of other children and asked them to choose whom they'd like to have as friends. Of the white children 86% picked children of their own race. When the kids were five and and six, Katz gave these children a small deck of cards, with drawings of people on them. Katz told the children to sort the cards into two piles any way they wanted. Only 16% of the kids used gender to split the piles. Another 16% used a variety of other factors, like the age or the mood of the people depicted. But 68% of the kids used race to split the cards, without any prompting.

In reporting her findings, Katz concluded: "I think it is fair to say that at no point in the study did the children exhibit the Rousseau-type of color-blindness that many adults expect." [Philosopher Jean-Jacques Rousseau believed that humans are born naturally compassionate to others and have to learn prejudice.]

The point Katz emphasizes is that during this period of our children's lives when we imagine it's most important to *not* talk about race is the very developmental period when children's minds are forming their first conclusions about race.

Several studies point to the possibility of developmental windows—stages when children's attitudes might be most amenable to change. During one experiment, teachers divided their students into groups of six kids, making sure each child was in a racially diverse group. Twice a week, for eight weeks, the groups met. Each child in a group had to learn a piece of the lesson and then turn around and teach it to the other five. The groups received a grade collectively. Then, the scholars watched the kids on the playground, to see if it led to more interaction cross-race. Every time a child played with another child at recess, it was noted—as was the race of the other child.

The researchers found this worked wonders on the first-grade children. Having been in the cross-race study groups led to significantly more cross-race play. But it made no difference on the third-grade children. It's possible that by third grade, when parents usually recognize it's safe to start talking a little about race, the developmental window has already closed.

| "Children believed that parents wanted them to play with a White rather than a Black peer."

Children Are Taught to Be Aware of Racial Differences

Luigi Castelli, Luciana Carraro, Silvia Tomolleri, and Antonella Amari

Luigi Castelli is an associate professor in the Department of Developmental Psychology and Socialization at the University of Padova in Italy. His research interests are personal behaviors within group identities, including those relating the transmission of racial attitudes within a family. The following viewpoint describes research on preschool-age children in Italy regarding their opinions of black or white children as playmates. The study revealed the strong influence of expectations about the race of their playmates the children think their parents have, and whether the children believe their parents would prefer to associate with black or white adults.

Luigi Castelli et al, "White Children's Alignment to the Perceived Racial Attitudes of the Parents: Closer to the Mother than the Father," *British Journal of Developmental Psychology*, vol. 25, September 2007, pp. 353–357. Reproduced with permission from The British Journal of Developmental Psychology. Copyright © The British Psychological Society.

As you read, consider the following questions:

1. How many children participated in the study discussed in the viewpoint?

2. What was the relationship between the children's ages and their likelihood of preferring a hypothetical black playmate, according to Castelli?

3. According to the research results, with which parent are children's attitudes toward hypothetical black and white playmates most affiliated?

There is an open debate in the literature about the role of parents in shaping the White children's interethnic attitudes. Indeed, empirical data are often contradictory. Very few studies found a positive correlation between White parents' and children's attitudes, but other studies failed to detect such a relation. Importantly, an effect of the White parents emerged only on their adolescent children, but it was never found in the case of preschoolers.

[Researchers Luigi] Castelli, [C.] Zogmaister, and [S.] Tomelleri argued that parents' verbal responses may be affected by social desirability concerns and self-presentation strategies, whereas preschool children's responses are not, and this may explain the lack of correlation between the two. Consistent with this hypothesis, data showed that White parents' responses to a prejudice questionnaire were not related to their 4–7-year-old children's attitudes, whereas the implicit attitude of the mother (but not of the father) was a significant predictor. Therefore, the White mothers appeared to play a relevant role in the socialization of racial attitudes. Similarly, [Megan] O'Bryan and colleagues found that mothers' racial attitudes were indeed more strongly correlated to their adolescent children's attitudes than fathers' attitudes were. Overall, the limited research in this area suggests that the maternal transmission of racial attitudes might be stronger than paternal transmission, at least in the case of attitudes towards Blacks.

In the present paper, we examined the differential influence of the two parents from a different perspective. We first measured the White children's attitudes towards Blacks and then we assessed children's beliefs about the attitudes held by their parents. In particular, we assessed what the children believed of parental expectations about how they should behave in interracial situations, and what they believed to be the personal interracial preferences of their parents. In this way, we could verify the relationship between the personal attitudes of the children and what they perceived to be the expectations and attitudes of their parents. It was predicted that children's attitudes would be more strongly related to the perceived expectations and attitudes of mothers than fathers.

The Study Parameters

Fifty-eight White children from 4 to 7 years of age participated in the study (30 females and 28 males). They all lived in southern Italy and had quite limited contact with the Blacks. Consent was obtained from parents.

Children were interviewed individually. They were shown drawings of a White and a Black child and they were first asked to choose a playmate. Secondly, the desire to play with each of the two targets was separately assessed along a 4-point scale ranging from 'not at all' to 'very much'. The relative order of the questions was counterbalanced across the participants. Thirdly, the children were then asked to attribute four positive (nice, happy, clean and likable) and four negative traits (ugly, sad, dirty and bad) to the two targets. Four response options were allowed and each trait could be assigned to the White child, to the Black child, to both of them or to neither of them.

Next, the children were invited to think about their mother and report whether she would have preferred that they played with the White or the Black child. The children were also asked how much they thought their mother would have been happy if they played with the White and the Black child. Responses were collected on a 4-point Likert scale [a rating scale that measures levels of agreement]. This same sequence of questions was repeated for fathers. The relative order of questions about mothers and fathers was counterbalanced across the participants.

Subsequently, the drawings of two female adults, one White and one Black, were presented. Participants were told that their mother had the chance to meet one of these two adults and they were asked to predict whom the mother would prefer to meet. The children were also asked to predict how the mother would have attributed the eight traits presented above. In order to simplify the task that requires foreseeing someone else's behaviour, two response options were allowed and each trait could be given either to the White or the Black adult. There was no constraint to give the same number of traits to the targets. The same procedure was repeated for fathers and predictions were made in relations to the drawings of two male adults. Again, the relative order of the questions was counterbalanced across the participants.

Finally, the respondents were thanked and returned to their class.

The Preschoolers' Responses

Personal Attitudes

As for the playmate choice, the majority of the respondents preferred the White (86%) rather than the Black playmate. The independent assessment of the desire to play with each of the two targets confirmed a preference for the ethnic in-group over the out-group. . . .

Learning To Be Prejudiced

Children are learning all the time. They learn from the attitudes and values of the people around them, including other children. Attitudes, including prejudiced attitudes, are not inborn—they are learned. They learn them from everything that is around them, including books, dolls, toys, videos and posters, from adults, other children and the media, in the following ways.

What children see (and don't see) If children rarely see black people and mixed race families in their books, jigsaw puzzles and posters, they may learn that they are not really part of our society. On television, if they see few women or black people in status roles they may learn to think that only white men can be in these positions.

What children hear (and don't hear) If a child is with her mum and they meet a friend who refers to 'dirty Pakis' [Pakistanis], the child may receive the message that it's all right to use the word 'Paki' and that such people are dirty—unless someone immediately, or very soon afterwards, explains that the term used by the friend is completely unacceptable and that Pakistan is a country in the same way as England. If no one ever mentions black people and they do not live in their area, children may think that black people only exist on the television, live only in 'rough' inner-city areas, play football or do not live anywhere in Britain.

What children do (and don't do) If a white mother makes it clear that her daughter's black friend will not be welcome at her birthday party then her daughter is unlikely to invite her. The mother will not have the opportunity to get to know her, her daughter will feel uncomfortable and her friend is likely to feel resentful, unhappy, excluded and possibly not know why she was not invited.

Jane Lane, Young Children and Racial Justice, *2008.*

Additional analyses showed that participant gender did not influence responses. As for participants' age, we found that respondents who chose a Black playmate tended to be younger than those who chose a White playmate. Similarly, the desire to play with a Black peer tended to decrease with age. These results are consistent with [Frances] Aboud's model which suggests that prejudice may increase between 4 and 7 years of age.

Perceived Expectations of the Parents

Participants perceived that mothers and fathers would have preferred them to choose a White playmate (83 and 81%, for mothers and fathers, respectively) rather than a Black playmate. Responses to the Likert scales provided consistent results. The children perceived that the mother would have been happier if they played with a White than a Black child. The same pattern emerged in relation to the perceived expectations of the father. No effect of participants' gender and age emerged.

Perceived Attitudes of the Parents

Children believed that their parents would have preferred to meet a White adult (74% for both mothers and fathers) rather than a Black adult. In addition, the mother was expected to give more positive than negative traits to the White adult. This implies that the Black adult received more negative than positive traits. Similarly, the father was also expected to give more positive than negative traits to the White adult. No effect of participants' gender and age emerged. . . .

Children Let Parents' Attitudes Shape Their Own

Results confirmed the presence of strong racial biases in the sample. A White target was indeed more likely to be chosen as a playmate than a Black target. Similarly, White children attributed more positive traits to the White than the Black target, whereas the opposite occurred for negative traits. Moreover, participants perceived that their parents also had prejudiced attitudes towards the Blacks and biased expectations. Indeed, the respondents had a clear perception about their parents' expectations. Children believed that parents wanted them to play with a White rather than a Black peer. This suggests that the young children in our sample perceived normative expectations which encourage in-group bias instead of condemning it.

However, the major interest was in the relation between perceived parents' expectations and attitudes on one hand and personal attitudes on the other hand. . . . The data clearly indicated that the children's attitudes were more closely related to what the children believed to be the attitudes and the expectations of their mothers than those of their fathers. These results are not consistent with the idea that respondents simply project their own attitudes onto parents. In contrast, a significant relation emerged only in the case of the mother. This specific relation supports from a different perspective idea that there is a stronger link between the White children's racial attitudes and the attitudes held by their mothers than those held by their fathers. In sum, mothers seem to play a more relevant role in comparison with fathers in shaping children's responses towards Blacks. Future research will have to determine the specific processes that lead to this predominant influence of the mother, and whether this extends to the perception of other stigmatized out-groups.

Periodical Bibliography

The following articles have been selected to supplement the diverse views presented in this chapter.

Sarah Avery   "Clue to Disease Rates in Genes," *News & Observer*, December 9, 2009.

Aravinda Chakravarti   "Kinship: Race Relations: Our Notions of Family, Population and Race May Need Revising in the Age of Personal Genomics," *Nature*, January 22, 2009.

Elizabeth Ellis   "Census Question on Race Doesn't Ask for the Truth About Humanity," *Minnesota Spokesman-Recorder*, June 2, 2010.

Amy Harmon   "In DNA Era, New Worries About Prejudice," *New York Times*, November 11, 2007.

John B. Judis   "Census Nonsense: Why Barack Obama Isn't Black," *The New Republic*, April 7, 2010.

Ziba Kashef   "Genetic Drift: The Study of Human Genes Has Sparked a Resurgence of Debate About the True Nature of Race," *Colorlines Magazine*, September–October 2007.

Philip Kitcher   "Does 'Race' Have a Future?" *Philosophy and Public Affairs*, Fall 2007.

P.C. NG et al.   "Individual Genomes Instead of Race for Personalized Medicine," *Clinical Pharmacology & Therapeutics*, September 2008.

Gina Miranda Samuels   "Building Kinship and Community: Relational Processes of Bicultural Identity Among Adult Multiracial Adoptees," *Family Process*, March 2010.

Olivier Uyttebrouk   "Founder Effect: Several Illnesses Seen in Hispanics Are Traced Back to Early Settlers in New Mexico," *Albuquerque Journal*, September 7, 2009.

OPPOSING
VIEWPOINTS®
SERIES

CHAPTER 2

How Does Society Impact Race Relations?

Chapter Preface

There is a plot afoot to cast black actor Donald Glover as the next Spider-Man. The movie franchise is due for another installment and his name was suggested in a comment on a blog and the idea garnered momentum. Glover has admitted that he does admire the character and would like to audition for the role, but does not expect to be automatically cast. He is a relatively unknown actor on a new sitcom, *Community*, so on basis of celebrity alone, he is hardly a shoo-in for the part. What makes this story interesting is the public opposition to the suggestion.

Spider-Man has always been portrayed as part spider, part white human. That is how creators Stan Lee and Steve Ditko imagined him in 1962 and it is how he has been cast ever since. Ardent comic book fans in opposition to the casting of Donald Glover believe in the authenticity of the character, and in staying faithful to origin stories. Peter Parker, Spider-Man's human identity, is white in the comic books and he is white in the television shows and he has been white in the movies. To some, putting a black actor in the role is taking an inexcusable liberty with who the character is. It is not a racist objection—it is a matter of literary faithfulness.

The theatrical musical *Miss Saigon* met a similar controversy when it opened in New York City in 1991. The role of the Eurasian character "Engineer" was played by known Broadway star Jonathan Pryce, a white actor who had originated the role in the London production. The Actors' Equity Association tried to block Pryce from playing the role on the grounds that it was inappropriate to cast against racial type. Supporters of Pryce pointed out that the character was written as half-white and half-Vietnamese, and that casting an Asian actor would be just as much "against" racial type as the white Pryce would be. That the Engineer is of mixed race is an essential feature of his character, and provides an explanation of sorts for why he works as a pimp (a low-status profession that requires frequent interaction with Americans) in 1970s Vietnam. Ultimately, the show opened with Pryce and other white actors have since been cast in the role.

The Marc Webb-directed *Spider-Man* film is scheduled to be released in 2012 by Sony Pictures Entertainment and Columbia Pictures. A joint announcement of the project from January 20, 2010, indicated the studios' interpretation of the tale and their confidence in Webb's ability to present it:

> At its core, *Spider-Man* is a small, intimate human story about an everyday teenager that takes place in an epic super-human world. . . . We wanted someone who could capture the awe of being in Peter's shoes so the audience could experience his sense of discovery while giving real heart to the emotion, anxiety, and recklessness of that age and coupling all of that with the adrenaline of Spider-Man's adventure.

What Spider-Man purists and Donald Glover fans are debating now is whether a black actor can be the protagonist of a "human story" about an "everyday teenager" and whether race is relevant to the "emotion, anxiety, and recklessness" that accompany the combination of being an adolescent and a super-hero in America. They are discussing whether "white" is Spider-Man's necessary default setting or just an artifact of the era in which he was born, whether "white" is an accidental happenstance, or an essential part of his character.

The following chapter portrays the challenges individuals face when their personal interests and desires conflict with expectations placed upon them because of their race, and how people's behavior is influenced by being part of a racially and ethnically diverse society.

│ *"Many people remain staunchly opposed*
│ *to interracial unions of any kind."*

Interracial Romances Are Not Well Accepted

Derek A. Kreager

Derek A. Kreager is an assistant professor of crime, law, and justice at Pennsylvania State University. His research interests are in adolescent development, particularly how adolescents' positions within their social networks influence their behavior and interests. The following viewpoint is from a paper that analyzed data from the National Longitudinal Study of Adolescent Health—a survey of thousands of adolescents regarding their physical, mental, and sexual health and behaviors—to investigate whether interracial dating was tolerated or discouraged among high school students. Kreager found that students in interracial relationships experienced disapproval and negative sanctions from their peers.

As you read, consider the following questions:

1. According to the author, what are some examples of cultural dimensions that help people define the terms and the boundaries of their group identities?

Derek A. Kreager, "Guarded Borders: Adolescent Interracial Romance and Peer Trouble at School," *Social Forces*, vol. 87, December 2008, pp. 887–905. Copyright © 2008 by the University of North Carolina Press. Used by permission.

2. What aspects of adolescent life, according to Kreager, may contribute to the premature end of interracial romantic relationships?

3. According to the author, what are three characteristics of disapproval to adolescent interracial romantic relationships?

R ace scholars have long viewed inter-group romantic partnerships as barometers of social equality. According to classic assimilation theory, rising numbers of interracial and interethnic unions represent the final stages of group assimilation and the erosion of barriers to social mobility. . . . Research in this vein consistently finds that American intermarriage rates have increased substantially over the past four decades, suggesting a relaxation of historically persistent social boundaries. However, authors are quick to point out that racially mixed marriages remain infrequent and have risen more rapidly for some racial groups than others. According to the 2000 U.S. Census, approximately 7 percent of the nation's 61.5 million married and cohabiting couples were racially mixed. This number falls well below random mixing expectations, with black-white marriages remaining particularly infrequent. The latter trend suggests that the symbolic and social barriers separating blacks and whites remain firmly entrenched in American society.

Scholars commonly link the infrequency of intermarriage to racially segregated communities or individual preferences for culturally similar companions. Often overlooked, however, are the effects that informal sanctions may have on early interracial relationships. Although formal barriers to intermarriage disappeared more than 40 years ago and attitudes toward these relationships have become increasingly tolerant, many people remain staunchly opposed to interracial unions of any kind. In a highly publicized 1997 Gallup poll, a majority of teenagers stated that they had dated someone of another race, demonstrating the general acceptance of interracial romances. However, another quarter of those surveyed stated that they would never consider dating interracially and would have a problem with those who did. The disapproving actions from the latter group may be enough to prematurely end a young, racially mixed romance, even for couples embedded in diverse friendship networks or integrated social settings. Negative peer reactions are particularly effective during the teenage years. With few opportunities for privacy or changed social environments, interracial adolescent couples are vulnerable to various kinds of social sanctions, including gossip, group exclusion and threats of violence.

This article explores the potential risks associated with adolescent interracial dating. Although numerous qualitative studies document the proscriptive sanctions aimed at interracial couples, quantitative research on this issue remains limited, reducing our ability to determine if young interracial couples are at greater risk of peer difficulties than intra-racial couples. In this study, I compare inter- and intra-racially dating adolescents on an index of school-based peer trouble taken from the National Longitudinal Study of Adolescent Health. Drawing on social-psychological research of inter-group relations, I hypothesize that involvement in an interracial relationship will increase problematic peer encounters. Normative pressures toward racial homophily [associating with people like you] increase the likelihood that third-parties will initiate "border patrolling" behaviors meant to dissuade interracial romances, particularly between blacks and non-blacks. Results from this research help to clarify the interracial romantic experience and identify a potential mechanism for continued low intermarriage rates.

Rigid Definitions of Group Identity

For decades, social psychologists have attended to issues of group identification and inter-group relations. According to

Distribution of Adolescent Romantic Relationships by Race of Respondent and Partner

Respondent's Race	Partner's Race					Total Number of Respondents
	White	Black	Hispanic	Asian	Other	
White	**3,685.0**	95.0	225.0	45.0	131.0	4,181.0
Percentage of total	**88.1**	2.3	5.4	1.1	3.1	55.7
Black	122.0	**1,371.0**	68.0	11.0	49.0	1,621.0
Percentage of total	7.5	**84.6**	4.2	0.7	3.0	21.6
Hispanic	253.0	73.0	**788.0**	31.0	89.0	1,234.0
Percentage of total	20.5	5.9	**63.9**	2.5	7.2	16.5
Asian	66.0	18.0	38.0	**228.0**	51.0	401.0
Percentage of total	16.5	4.5	9.5	**56.9**	12.7	5.3
Other	23.0	17.0	14.0	8.0	**2.0**	64.0
Percentage of total	35.9	26.6	21.9	12.5	**3.1**	0.9
Total number of partners	4,149.0	1,574.0	1,133.0	323.0	322.0	7,501.0
Percentage of total	55.3	21.0	15.1	4.3	4.3	100.0

TAKEN FROM: Derek Kreager, *Social Forces*, 2008.

social identity theory, individuals seek to increase their self-concepts by favorably evaluating their own group memberships relative to other groups. This process of differentiation results in feelings of superiority for "in-group" members and less favorable evaluations of those in "out-groups." When combined with historical inequities and inter-group competition, in-group biases foster discrimination by high-status individuals toward low-status groups, thereby hardening negative group stereotypes and perceptions of boundary impermeability. However, in-group preference and out-group stereotyping are not confined to high status individuals. Symbolic boundaries based on cultural and normative dimensions—such as language, music, dress, values, religion, etc.—provide avenues for low-status individuals to resist dominant group stereotypes and positively define their own collective identities. Thus, tendencies toward group distinction and in-group favoritism arise regardless of groups' social statuses, creating intergroup boundaries that are often difficult to cross.

When group social distances are large and boundaries appear impermeable, individuals with cross-group ties pose problems for those loyal to one group. In such instances, border crossing challenges established perceptions of group superiority or group distinction. Interracial romantic relationships have historically fallen in this category. Whites may perceive such relationships as endangering white privilege, particularly in times of economic insecurity. [Researcher Michelle] Fine et al. document this phenomenon in their ethnography of white working-class boys. The boys in their study directed economic frustrations at black males, who were portrayed as sexually encroaching on white girls. Protecting white women from black "contamination" provided the white boys a means of reasserting their racial superiority and constructing valued masculine identities, both of which were threatened in a period of neighborhood economic decline.

Black females may also hold strong objections to black male-white female relationships. Black females often view these relationships as rejections of the black community and the beauty of black women. Similar to working-class white boys, black females' objections commonly originate from perceived inequality in the social structure. For many black women, unions between black males and white females symbolize the abandonment of black families that are already besieged by poverty and mass incarceration. With negative evaluations emanating from both racial categories, negotiating a black-white interracial romance is likely to be particularly problematic. And although the black-white divide remains the most visible racial boundary in modern America, negative evaluations of any interracial romance are likely to occur whenever racial groups are socially distant and inter-group competition is high.

Interracial Romances Are Typically Short-lived

The early dissolution of interracial romances due to social sanctions or "border patrolling" behaviors may explain tendencies for interracial daters and cohabiters to exit mixed relationships prior to marriage. Hostility and exclusionary practices felt by young interracial couples pose serious obstacles to sustained relationships, potentially "winnowing" interracial romances from the dating-to-marriage path. Third-party sanctions would be particularly effective at discouraging adolescent interracial romances, as young interracial daters would be forced to simultaneously negotiate emerging sexual identities, precarious peer-group positions and negative social evaluations. Moreover, adolescents have limited control over their social environments, leaving few opportunities to avoid problematic peer encounters. Their homes, schools and communities are all chosen for them and are unlikely to change should problems arise. Adolescents involved in interracial romances would then have few options to avoid negative encounters, and the options open to them (i.e., dropout, repressed anger, notifying officials or retaliation) are likely to decrease rather than increase relationship stability and future cross-race contacts.

Adding to the complexity of a young interracial romance is the racial demarcation that typically accompanies secondary education. Developmental researchers commonly find racial homophily to be a defining characteristic of mid-adolescent friendship networks. Academic tracking, busing, increased awareness of community and parental backgrounds, and the search for racial identity all contribute to highly segregated school environments. Within these contexts, interracial romances become visible threats to the status quo and potentially activate third-party sanctions meant to dissuade such relationships. . . .

Strong Peer Relationships vs. Interracial Romance

Although greater tolerance for interracial unions exists today than in the past, racially mixed relationships remain infrequent. This infrequency may be partially explained by the social risks facing young interracial couples. In this study, I found that involvement in an interracial relationship significantly increased adolescents' perceptions of peer problems at school. These results are consistent with the hypothesis, derived from social identity theory and ethnographic accounts, that interracial couples face substantial obstacles in daily interactions. Although by no means definitive, this study provides quantitative evidence for the difficulties that accompany interracial dating.

I also found that the effect of interracial dating on negative social encounters varied by the race of the dater. Blacks in interracial romances perceived the greatest peer trouble, while Asians and Hispanics showed little differences from their intra-racial dating peers. Indeed, Asian interracial daters were predicted to have *fewer* peer troubles than Asian intra-racial daters. These patterns likely stem from heightened perceptions of norm violation associated with black/non-black romances. Hidden racial prejudices may become activated by these interracial relationships, and exposure to prejudice appears to be greatest for the black member of the interracial couple.

Given the infrequency of interracial dating, it is possible that individuals choosing to enter such relationships are inherently risk-takers. A propensity for risk may then explain the effects observed in this study, in that risk-taking could increase rates of negative social encounters. . . .

Interviews of interracial couples and evidence from school ethnographies suggest that disapproval (1. is frequently subtle and non-violent, (2. comes from peers outside of the daters' social networks, and (3. often originates from same-race peers. The resulting picture is one of young interracial daters facing often unidentifiable or generalized disapproval from school-based peers. In racially homogeneous or highly segregated schools, interracial romances would potentially upset the delicate social balance and prompt immediate responses. Faced with intolerance, interracial daters may either distance themselves from school-based peers or choose to end the relationship and avoid stigmatization. Examining the latter possibility would be an excellent topic for future research.

> "The differences that had to do with his being Maori . . . were considered extremely interesting, while anything that could be construed as a working-class mannerism . . . was quietly frowned upon."

Social Class Differences Are Less Tolerable than Racial Differences in Romance

Christina Thompson

Christina Thompson is the editor of the literary journal, Harvard Review. *Her essays and articles have appeared in numerous other publications, including* Vogue, American Scholar, *the* Journal of Pacific History, *and* Australian Literary Studies. *The following viewpoint describes her cross-cultural marriage to a native New Zealander, which perplexed people not because this white woman had married a brown man but because this highly educated New England academic had married a worker with an impoverished background from a lower social class. She argues that generally people are expected to "marry up," and that her decision not to caused frequent dismay.*

As you read, consider the following questions:

1. What does the author claim is the difference between expectations about class and expectations about cultural differences?

2. What did Thompson believe she was personally immune to?

3. Why was the author so upset when her husband accepted a door-to-door salesman job?

In the early years of our marriage, people always used to ask us how we'd met. It was not in itself an unusual question, but there was always an edge of genuine perplexity whenever it was put to us. You could tell that people really did wonder how two paths as divergent as ours could have crossed. It's not just a matter of how we look; it's everything about us. I am a small, fair-haired New Englander; my husband, Seven, is a six-foot-two, 200-pound Polynesian. I have a Ph.D.; he went to trade school. I edit *Harvard Review*; he manufactures tools for a living. . . .

I grew up in a little town on the outskirts of Boston, where if I poked around in the oldest churchyards I could always find a gravestone with one or the other of my family names. My father was an economist; my mother was a painter; both of my grandfathers had been engineers. Summers we traveled to Europe, where I visited museums with my mother while my father taught, and read a great deal, especially Victorian novels. By the time I was ten I was so well traveled that, even now, if I picture myself as a child, it is not in the woods or fields of New England but on a bridge in Paris in a coat the color of daffodils and patent leather shoes. My husband, on the other hand, is a "native," whose ancestors arrived in canoes from central Polynesia sometime in the first millennium A.D. Toward the mid-nineteenth century New Zealand was annexed by the British crown, and since then the fate of the

Maori has mirrored that of many other indigenous peoples. Mostly displaced and disempowered, they generally occupy the lower strata of society, with higher rates of unemployment, poorer health, and lower levels of educational achievement than white New Zealanders. My husband's family was comparatively lucky in that they retained a fragment of their tribal land. He grew up in a rural community in which everyone was not only Maori but, in some way or another, related to him. They still lived, to a large extent, on seafood that they caught; they still wove flax kits and baskets; they still spoke the language of their ancestors at home. That said, they were extremely poor. My husband's father worked any number of jobs, often far from home, building houses, picking fruit. His mother raised ten children in a four-room house with rudimentary plumbing. Until my husband's generation, no one in the family had been educated beyond high school; many in the previous generation had not reached that. My husband swears that he was ten years old before he owned a pair of shoes, and when I look at the width of his feet, I can believe it.

Class Aspirations and Expectations

People think that marrying across ethnic or racial lines is difficult, but in my experience, the trickier thing is marrying across class. The barriers are formidable: People from different classes have different ways of doing things, different values, different bodies of knowledge, different expectations about the world. They belong, effectively, to different cultures, but unlike the cultures associated with race or ethnicity or religion, class is something you are supposed to want to change. No matter where you fall in the socioeconomic hierarchy (unless you are already at the absolute top), you are expected to aspire to something better: working to middle class, middle to upper-middle. Even the language is unambiguous: "upper" and "lower"; "climbing" the social ladder; social "advancement";

"improving" one's lot. And so, while it is comparatively easy to be evenhanded about other kinds of cultural differences—who is ready to say that Judaism, for example, is "better" than Christianity? Or that it is objectively "better" to be Polish than Greek?—it is almost impossible to be truly neutral about class.

I could see how true this was within my own family. My mother's family had been wealthier and better positioned socially than that of my father, and culturally we followed my mother's lead, aiming "up" at the highest social level to which we could plausibly aspire. At the same time, we were politically liberal. My father was a populist, and my mother had been a Socialist in her youth, and both were broadly tolerant people. What this meant, as far as my husband was concerned, was tricky. On the one hand, he was popular with my family, who admired his genial nature and easy ways. At the same time it always struck me that the differences that had to do with his being Maori (his unwillingness to leave any part of a fish uneaten, even the eyes and brains, for example) were considered extremely interesting, while anything that could be construed as a working-class mannerism (like watching TV in the daytime or wearing his baseball cap indoors) was quietly frowned upon.

I found all this fascinating from a sociological point of view. I had always been curious about other people and interested in anything different from what I knew. It was one of the things that had attracted me to my husband in the first place, what had drawn me to his far-flung corner of the world. I flattered myself that I was immune to these socially constructed prejudices, regardless of whether they arose from differences of ethnicity, race, religion, or social class. And then, one day, quite by accident, I came face-to-face with a set of feelings that, if you had asked me, I would certainly have denied having had.

Race, Gender, Career, and the Balance of Power

Warren saw nothing particularly remarkable about his involvement in an interracial relationship because he was "raised to appreciate all people." As he explained it,

> My family is real open-minded about things like that. There's no color lines in my family at all ... None of my friends have had any problems either because in the neighborhood I grew up in, everything was pretty interracial. My parents always ... I mean I was raised up in interracial relationships all the way through. The neighborhood I grew up in was that way. If there were any problems, I wasn't aware of it. ...

Warren noted that when he was out with his partner, there were often uncomfortable reactions from others. He recalled that if he pointed it out to her she was "usually totally oblivious to their reactions and could have cared less."

Kellina Craig-Henderson,
Black Men in Interracial Relationships, *2006.*

Confronted with Her Own Prejudices

We had been married for about five years when my husband and and I moved to a city where, for the first time, he had difficulty finding employment. I had been awarded a fellowship at the local university and was supporting a family of four—me, my husband, our first child, and my husband's youngest sister, who had come to live with us—on a postdoctoral stipend. It was, therefore, imperative that my husband get some kind of work. He'd had a number of different jobs in the past: dispatching cars, casting boat parts, riding as a bicycle messenger—but none of these was an option in the place where we now lived. He talked about becoming a taxi driver and worked for a while as a janitor in a factory where they made salads for supermarket chains. He did a brief stint as a builder's laborer, and then one day he came home and told me that he had taken a job selling vacuum cleaners door to door.

I still have difficulty explaining the effect this announcement had on me, but it was a bit like being dropped into a cold, dark well. At the time, I didn't even understand my reaction; I just knew I couldn't tolerate the idea, and I begged him to go back and tell them he'd decided against taking the job. My husband thought I was being unreasonable. There was nothing about the job, he argued, that made it any worse or better than any of the other things he'd ever done. In fact, it was a lot easier than cycling and cleaner than foundry work. But nothing he could say made any difference, because my reasons for feeling the way I did were, in fact, entirely irrational, arising as they did from something I'd experienced as a child.

When I was growing up, a traveling salesman paid a visit to my parents' house once or twice a year. He had a large old car and a shabby coat, and he came in the late fall or early spring, so that it was always damp and cold whenever I saw him. I still have a vivid image of the way he looked, with his rounded shoulders and his heavy case, and of the way he shuffled across the gravel to our front door. I felt quite sad about this man and also a bit scared of him, but mostly what I felt was guilt. It was clear to me that there was something pitiful about him, that no one would want to do what he was doing out there in the drizzle while we were snug and warm in our nice home. And so, when my husband told me that he had taken a job as a door-to-door salesman, the shadow of this man washed over me, and for the first time in our marriage, I wondered what I had done.

Until that point, I had viewed my husband's various occupations with humor and something like pride. There was a certain masculine integrity in being a bicycle messenger, for example, or a machinist. I never cared that he wasn't white-collar. My own work was like a parody of professional employment (I still haven't had a job outside a university), and it always seemed to me that it was sensible to have someone in the family who was good with his hands. But selling, particularly this dodgy variety, did not fit into any of these acceptable categories, and it was only the greatest of mercies that my husband proved inept at selling and, after a couple of weeks of pointless demonstrations, voluntarily gave it up.

A More Tolerant Future for Her Children

This episode crossed a line that, like a buried electrical cable, I hadn't known was there. If the idea of selling vacuum cleaners was humiliating, the fact that I was embarrassed by it was almost worse. I was not, as it turned out, completely open-minded, and it was humbling for me to realize that there were, in fact, places I didn't want to go. For years I had been blithely joking about sliding down the social ladder, as if none of the anxieties that worried other people could ever have applied to me. And yet here I was, unnerved by the prospect of being associated—even in the remotest and most obscure way—with that dismal little man. It was an absurd and at the same time salutary discovery that made me more honest about both what I expected of my husband and, even more important, what I envisioned for our children.

I had always felt that it was good for them to have parents from different social classes. I thought it would make them less snobbish and more tolerant of others and that it would give them a wider angle on the world. It was clear to me that, thanks to my upbringing, there was little to no chance they would grow up with a working-class identity like their father's. More likely, as had been the case in my own family, they would see themselves as belonging to some faded version of their mother's world. But what I truly hoped for, what I still hope for, is that they will end up someplace comparatively neutral. I like to think they might ultimately have social identities as fluid-seeming as the way they look, with their black eyes and brown hair and varying shades of skin. Ethnically indeterminate, difficult to place, they are, in my fondest dream of their imaginary future, unconstrained by membership in any social class.

> "A lot of employers would rather not deal with black American workers if they have the option of hiring a docile Hispanic immigrant instead."

Latino Immigrants Take Jobs from African Americans

Cord Jefferson

Cord Jefferson is a regular contributor to The Root, *a daily online magazine that provides commentary on current issues from a variety of black perspectives. He also has written for* The Huffington Post, National Geographic, *and* The Onion. *The following viewpoint argues against the belief that illegal immigrants, especially Latino immigrants, take the jobs that Americans do not want. Jefferson provides evidence to demonstrate that African Americans work in large numbers in these "undesirable" industries—from meat processing and food service to building maintenance—and offers alternate explanations for why illegal immigrants are more likely to be hired in those fields.*

Cord Jefferson, "How Illegal Immigration Hurts Black America," *The Root*, February 10, 2010. Reproduced by permission of the author.

As you read, consider the following questions:

1. According to the author, what evidence suggests that African Americans are, in fact, willing to do the jobs that have been thought of as only acceptable to illegal immigrants?

2. According to Jefferson, what was the median household income for illegal immigrants in 2007?

3. Why does Vanderbilt law professor Carol Swain believe that black scholars have remained silent on the relationship between illegal immigration and African American unemployment rates?

In October 2008, amidst claims that one of its subsidiaries was knowingly hiring illegal immigrants, North Carolina poultry producer House of Raeford Farms initiated a systematic conversion of its workforce.

Following a U.S. Immigration and Customs Enforcement raid that nabbed 300 undocumented workers at a Columbia Farms processing plant in Columbia, S.C., a spooked House of Raeford quietly began replacing immigrants with native-born labor at all of its plants. Less than a year later, House of Raeford's flagship production line in Raeford, N.C., had been transformed, going from more than 80 percent Latino to 70 percent African-American, according to a report by the *Charlotte Observer*.

Under President George W. Bush, showy workplace raids like the one that befell Raeford were standard—if widely despised—fare. And though the [Barack] Obama administration has committed itself to dialing down the practice, Homeland Security Secretary Janet Napolitano has occasionally found herself the bearer of bad news to immigration activists who expected the raids to end entirely under her watch.

For the most part, the workplace crackdowns themselves are unremarkable—gaudy, *ad hoc* things that mitigate

America's immigration problem the way a water balloon might a forest fire. Increasingly however, their immediate aftermaths—in which dozens of eager African-American job applicants line up to fill vacancies—call into question a familiar refrain from the nation's more vocal immigration proponents: Illegal immigrants do work American citizens won't. Even former Mexican President Vicente Fox fell victim to the hype, infamously declaring in 2006 that Mexican immigrants perform the jobs that "not even blacks want to do."

Americans Do Want These Jobs

Four years later, with national unemployment hovering around 10 percent and black male unemployment at a staggering 17.6 percent, it seems even less likely that immigrants are filling only those jobs that Americans won't deign to do. Just ask Delonta Spriggs, a 24-year-old black man profiled in a November *Washington Post* piece on joblessness, who pleaded, "Give me a chance to show that I can work. Just give me a chance."

Spriggs has a difficult road ahead. In this recessed United States, competition for all work is dog-eat-dog. But that holds especially true for low-skilled jobs, jobs for which high school dropouts (like Spriggs) and reformed criminals (also like Spriggs) must now vie against nearly 12 million illegal immigrants, 80 percent of whom are from Latin America. What's more, it seems that, in many cases, the immigrants are winning. From 2007 to 2008, though Latino immigrants reported significant job losses, black unemployment, the worst in the nation, remained 3.5 points higher.

"I don't believe there are any jobs that Americans won't take, and that includes agricultural jobs," says Carol Swain, professor of law at Vanderbilt University and author of *Debating Immigration*. "[Illegal immigration] hurts low-skilled, low-wage workers of all races, but blacks are harmed the most because they're disproportionately low-skilled."

Despite [Mexican] President Fox's assertion, of the Pew Hispanic Center's top six occupational sectors for undocumented immigrants (farming, maintenance, construction, food service, production and material moving), all six employed hundreds of thousands of blacks in 2008. That year, almost 15 percent of meat-processing workers were black, as were more than 18 percent of janitors. And although blacks on the whole aren't involved in agriculture at anywhere near the rates of illegal immigrants—a quarter of whom work in farming—about 14 percent of fruit and vegetable sorters are African-American.

Employers Prefer Illegal Immigrants

For their efforts, African Americans were paid a median household income of $32,000 in 2007. In the same year, the median household income for illegal immigrants was $37,000.

Audrey Singer is a senior fellow specializing in race and immigration at the Brookings Institution. She agrees that blacks are disproportionately hindered by illegal immigration, but says that pay is a necessary variable to note when talking about work Americans will and won't do. "There is evidence that shows people at the lower end of the skill spectrum are most affected by immigrant labor, particularly illegal immigrant labor," she says. "But would Americans do the jobs illegal workers do at the wages that they're paid? I don't think so."

Besides competing for work while simultaneously attempting to avoid drastically deflated paychecks and benefits, unemployed African-American job seekers must also frequently combat racial discrimination. In a 2006 research paper called "Discrimination in Low-Wage Labor Markets," a team of Princeton [University] sociologists discovered that, all else being equal, black applicants to low-wage jobs were 10 percent less likely than Latinos to receive positive responses from potential employers. Furthermore, employers were twice as likely to prefer white applicants to equally qualified blacks.

"To be blunt, a lot of employers would rather not deal with black American workers if they have the option of hiring a docile Hispanic immigrant instead," says Mark Krikorian, executive director of the Center for Immigration Studies. Krikorian's organization advocates a large-scale contraction of immigration to America, one of the main reasons being that low-skilled immigrants aren't contributing to the U.S. labor force in a way that American citizens can't. Nevertheless, Krikorian says that easily exploitable immigrants remain attractive to businesses looking to eliminate hassles. "[Illegal immigrants] are not going to demand better wages, and they're not going to ask for time off," he adds. "And frankly, a lot of bosses are thinking, 'I don't want to deal with a young black male.'"

Time for a National Discussion

Most political analysts expect the debate over immigration reform to find new life in 2010, under a president who thoughtfully supports both increased border enforcement and the "recognition of immigrants' humanity." Wherever the discussion meanders, however—from amnesty on the left to expulsion on the right—from here on, it seems that anyone interested in speaking thoroughly on the matter can no longer do so without discussing its impact on black America.

This type of discussion has proved difficult in the past, however. "Many of the black scholars dance around this hard issue," says Swain. "They do their research in such a way that it doesn't address how immigration affects blacks. There's a lot of pressure to say the politically correct thing—that immigrants aren't hurting African Americans. Well, that's not true."

> *"Black and white native-born workers seemed either not to notice or to give much weight to the changing faces of their coworkers."*

Latino Immigrants Easily Integrate with African Americans in the Work Force

Jamie Winders

Jamie Winders is an assistant professor of geography in the Maxwell School of Citizenship and Public Affairs at Syracuse University. The following viewpoint appears as an essay in the book New Faces in New Places, *which explores the geographical and social movements of immigrants, and the political and cultural response to their presence by native-born Americans. Winders examines in particular the effect of Latino immigration on Nashville, Tennessee, and contrasts the public image of racial conflict and economic competition to the ease with which individual immigrants and native-born Americans integrate personally and professionally in the workplace.*

As you read, consider the following questions:

1. According to Winders, what prompted Hotel Nashville to turn to Latino immigrants for new hires in the 1990s?

2. What aspects of working in the laundry room promote racial and ethnic workplace integration, according to the author?

3. According to Winders, how do the black and white native-born workers at the Hotel Nashville view the increasing numbers of Latino workers differently than do city and public officials?

"Everyone starts in housekeeping," remarked Janice, an Eastern European refugee and now a housekeeping supervisor, who began her tenure at Hotel Nashville as a room attendant in the mid-1990s. "Everyone," in Janice's comment, referred to a fifty-member workforce that reflects the multicultural, multilingual, and multi-ethnic realities of contemporary low-wage work sites across the United States. As recently as the 1980s, Hotel Nashville's workforce was composed primarily of African American women. In the late 1980s, however, the hotel, like others in the city [Nashville, Tenn.], began to see racial and ethnic transitions in its labor force, which followed the waves of refugees coming to Nashville initially from Southeast Asia and later from a variety of global hot spots. By the late 1990s, increasing numbers of Latino workers, particularly Mexican women, were joining this stream of workers at Hotel Nashville. During this time period, when labor shortages drove some Nashville hotels to fly in room cleaners from other cities, Hotel Nashville turned to Latino labor to avoid siphoning off workers from other hotels and "outbidding" their competitors by paying higher wages.

Hotel Nashville's current workforce includes white and black workers from Nashville and other American cities, Latino workers from Mexico and elsewhere in Latin America, and political refugees from around the world. Among this collection of employees are Mexican women who bring no formal work experience to their jobs, African American women who bring almost two decades of housekeeping experience, refugees who held government office jobs in their home countries, and Mexican men who have worked at low-wage work sites in Nashville and beyond. As Janice went on to stress in her comments, in housekeeping "it doesn't matter if you're educated or not." What matters is a willingness to do physically demanding and repetitive actions in room after room, day after day, in what [authors] Roger Waldinger and Michael Lichter describe as the best example of "dead-end jobs." In Hotel Nashville, "everyone" may start in housekeeping; but as this study showed, some, particularly older African American women, end up staying there.

The Public Dialogue About Racial Conflict

For six weeks in the spring of 2003, I spent my afternoons in Hotel Nashville's break room, interviewing and observing workers and supervisors in groups and individually. I asked what workers and supervisors thought about their department's rapid demographic shift and the arrival of a growing Latino workforce. How did hospitality workers interpret the changes that had caught social-service agencies and government officials so off guard and had reconfigured portions of Nashville's urban fabric and politics? What did Nashville's shifting racial and ethnic composition look like to Latino and other workers laboring in the city? . . .

In asking questions about work experiences in the hotel and elsewhere and in observing daily interactions at Hotel Nashville itself, I began to see a fairly consistent downplaying of the importance of demographic changes on daily workplace activities. When I asked native-born workers about the biggest changes they had seen in their tenure in housekeeping—which for some stretched back almost twenty years—they rarely mentioned their department's ethnic and racial change. When I asked Latino immigrant workers to compare their work experiences in Nashville to their work experience elsewhere, I received a variety of answers that offered glimpses into the effects of a more structured American workplace on older Mexican men or, for newly single Mexican women, the simultaneously liberating and limiting experiences of being working mothers. These responses, however, like those of native-born workers, rarely mentioned the different racial and ethnic composition in American, as compared to Mexican, work sites.

This pattern surprised me, given preliminary reports of workplace conflicts involving Latino workers in southern communities. To make sense of Hotel Nashville's seeming ill fit with these arguments, I turned to the hotel's microgeography of work. Various workplace studies have shown that the geographies of the workplace itself—the ways specific tasks are structured and performed spatially and the ways that workers encounter one another in the process of completing these tasks—powerfully affect workplace social interactions.

Within Hotel Nashville, the crew of room attendants is by far the largest and most ethnically diverse segment of housekeeping, with Mexican, Bosnian, Haitian, African American, and white female (and a few male) workers. This diversity, however, does not always translate into a racially or ethnically interactive workforce. Room attendants typically work alone in the hotel, as they clean a set number of rooms each day. Despite the fact that some room attendants work together and help one another on slow days and in cases of illness, ethnicity and race often contour who helps whom and in what language workplace conversation is conducted. Thus, the multicultural mix of room attendants at Hotel Nashville does not necessarily translate into a socially integrated and cohesive workforce. Instead, the combination of a labor geography of spatially separate and discrete rooms to be cleaned and a labor structure of individual room attendants assigned to particular rooms and floors reproduces a racially and ethnically separated, if not divided, workforce in the midst of marked diversity.

Multiethnic Cooperation and Integration

Among Hotel Nashville's laundry attendants, by contrast, Colombian, Mexican, and African American workers spend almost the entire day working side by side in a tight work space. Consequently, they are more dependent on mutual understanding to complete their assigned tasks. Through the spatial and social structure of their work, laundry attendants had a different experience of workplace diversity than did room attendants, and thus developed more extensive relationships across linguistic, cultural, and ethnic boundaries. Furthermore, these relationships often continued outside both the laundry room and the workday itself, as laundry workers interacted socially more than did room attendants.

For example, Beto, a young Mexican man from Guerrero, first encountered African Americans in the hotel's laundry room. In the laundry room, language is more important for workers than it is among room attendants, because verbal communication among laundry workers affects the pace of work in a department expected to produce a constant flow of clean linen. According to one worker, the laundry room is "the most hectic [space] in housekeeping;" and constantly switching between English, Spanish, and hand gestures can slow down work. For Beto, thus, black coworkers became a primary source of job, as well as English-language, training.

In the laundry room, informal interaction and learning takes place frequently and is central to the work itself. As Spanish- and English-speaking workers find a common language to sort the laundry, they also sort out cultural differences between *los mexicanos* and *los colombianos*. Learning to navigate such cultural differences is a key aspect of learning to negotiate new social relations at the workplace. Just as supervisors have had to learn to manage an increasingly multilingual, multiethnic, and multicultural workforce, some workers have had to do the same. In the hotel laundry room, such processes facilitate the completion of work in ways not found—perhaps because not so necessary—among the more ethnically diverse but also more structurally and spatially separate room attendants.

These microgeographies of race, ethnicity, and labor at Hotel Nashville clearly influence social interactions among workers and create a hypervisibility of Latino workers in areas like room cleaning and a relative invisibility elsewhere in the hotel. The spatial structure of work, however, is only part of the story. Since many employees at Hotel Nashville worked elsewhere before taking their current positions, their experiences at the hotel are always understood vis-à-vis [in terms of] previous work experiences. This led me to initiate conversations about how working at Hotel Nashville compared to working elsewhere, particularly in terms of the differences between current and former coworkers, to tease out how workers understood Nashville's new *sonido* ["sound" in Spanish] in comparison to its old sound.

Demographic Changes Go Unnoticed

In these conversations, many black and white native-born workers seemed either not to notice or to give much weight to the changing faces of their coworkers. For example, Evelyn, a young African American woman who had worked at Hotel Nashville for four years, described her current coworkers and her former coworkers at a laundry-processing facility in Nashville as "about the same—black and white in both places." This comment, variations of which were offered by other workers, raises the possibility that for some African American workers, "white" has become a catch-all category for nonblack workers, Latinos included. Further research on how racial cat-

Immigrants Are a Vital National Resource

Immigration is filling in gaps in the American workforce across the skills spectrum—from the lowest skilled jobs to the highest skilled fields.

Between 1980 and 2000, the proportion of native-born workers with high school and college degrees increased significantly, and the quality of the domestic labor force rose dramatically. Educational attainment will continue to increase, but the skill levels of the domestic labor force will not grow nearly as much. There will be fewer native-born workers available for low-skilled jobs due both to the demography of aging, and higher educational levels among native-born workers.

Immigration complements labor market gaps very well. High-skilled workers are a critical resource for a knowledge-driven economy. This is especially so in science and engineering, which have high concentrations of immigrants. At the same time, 11 of the 15 occupations projected to have the largest absolute job growth between 2004 and 2014 require less than a bachelor's degree. While about one-quarter of the foreign-born in the United States have a bachelor's degree or more, one-third have not completed high school, and thus become the labor pool for the hundreds of thousands of essential jobs that require relatively few skills.

From the standpoint of economic growth and competitiveness, building a system that taps the contributions of both high- and low-skilled immigrants is an asset for the nation.

Doris Meissner et al.,
Immigration and America's Future: A New Chapter, *2006.*

egories such as "white" are defined differently by various racial and ethnic groups is needed; but this comment points to the shifting processes through which Latino workers may be rendered invisible as "Latino" by their inclusion in the category "white" or by their wholesale removal from the workplace's racial grammar by native-born workers in new-immigrant destinations.

As I changed my questions to be more explicit about what workplace changes interested me; as I asked more questions about how participants' work experiences had changed over time; and as I sometimes pointed out changes that I thought were obvious (such as that participants' coworkers were all native-born at one hotel and now were a mixture of Mexicans, Colombians, Bosnians, and Americans), it became increasingly clear that these demographic changes may not have been so visible or so meaningful for hospitality workers as they were for city officials and community leaders. Instead of framing the entry of Latinos into the work site as a significant event, some workers used phrasing that echoed cultural-sensitivity training used in contemporary work sites. For example, Tonya, a black room attendant, remarked, "It's better to have a diverse workforce." Violet, an African-American lobby attendant, stated that at a "multicultural work site, you can learn more." Abby, a young white woman in rooms control, described her current work situation as much better than other places she had worked because "here, there is a diverse staff, which makes for a better work site." Perhaps most important, a surprising number of workers only referred to these demographic changes when I pressed the issue. When multiple workers remarked that current and former work experiences were "basically the same," I began to consider the possibility that in Hotel Nashville, Latino migration carried a different meaning and import than it did in Nashville's public sphere and that this difference was wrapped up with the difference that space and place make in understandings and practices of race and ethnicity. . . .

Workers and Politicians React Differently to Demographic Changes

[Historian] Raymond Mohl has argued that "blacks and Hispanics have been at odds over jobs, neighborhoods, and cultural differences for almost a decade" in the South. Citing academic and newspaper reports of a "tension-filled shop-floor situation" in North Carolina, Mohl notes that "as a consequence of recent Hispanic migration, new patterns of racial and ethnic conflict linger unresolved throughout the South." While not disputing these claims, I echo arguments from recent ethnographic work to suggest that representations of ethnic conflict in public discourse and the lived realities of these relations at a more intimate scale are not always congruent. In southern cities such as Nashville, the complexities of racial and ethnic interactions sit uneasily within broad-brush claims about definite regional trends, not least because these patterns of ethnic and racial conflict and coalition are still under design and discussion.

At the work sites I examined across the city, instead of generating strong inter-ethnic conflict or even interaction, the new realities of a multicultural, multilingual, and multiethnic work site were in some cases no more transformative than the arrival of new equipment. Within these sites, workplace social encounters seemed to follow . . . a "superficial politeness" among workers spatially proximate but socially distant. This is not to minimize what has been a dramatic transition in Nashville's low-wage labor market in the last ten years. Even if Latino and non-Latino workers did not attribute a great deal of significance to the racial and ethnic shifts across these work sites, almost all agreed that these transitions have changed how work gets done at each site, and other studies of immigrant experiences in Nashville point to hostile work environments, particularly for refugees.

What did not surface in this study was the sense that a new racial and ethnic composition at work sites mattered in the same way that such changes mattered within Nashville's public sphere. What was described as an "explosion" across the city appeared more like an ongoing process of coming to grips with changing workers at the workplace, where room attendants continued to have to clean the same numbers of rooms each day, orders still had to be filled as quickly as possible, and supervisors still had to find ways to help workers do their jobs. Although it is too early in the process of incorporating Latino workers into the local labor force in new-immigrant destinations to draw firm conclusions about how this incorporation will proceed in terms of ethnic and racial relations and formations, the differences to which this chapter points raise questions about the similarities and differences between workplace relations and public discourse in new immigrant-receiving cities such as the Music City [Nashville] and those documented in gateway cities such as Los Angeles.

Periodical Bibliography

The following articles have been selected to supplement the diverse views presented in this chapter.

Tresa Baldas   "Workers Challenge English-Only Rules,"
                      Fulton County Daily Report, June 15, 2007.

Sara Corbett   "A Prom Divided," *New York Times*, May 21,
                      2009.

Tony Dokoupil   "Raising Katie: What Adopting a White Girl
                      Taught a Black Family about Race in the
                      Obama Era," *Newsweek*, April 23, 2009.

Daisy Khan   "Balancing Tradition and Pluralism," *Sojourners
                      Magazine*, February 2009.

Cole Moreton   "England's Daft and Pleasant Land," *The
                      Guardian* (UK), February 12, 2010.

Eugene Robinson   "A Question of Race vs. Class," *Washington
                      Post*, May 15, 2007.

Elizabeth Stearns,   "Interracial Friendships in the Transition to
Claudia Buchmann,   College: Do Birds of a Feather Flock Together
and Kara Bonneau   Once They Leave the Nest?" *Sociology of
                      Education*, April 2009.

Carol Swain   "Apply Compassion Offered Illegal Immigrants
                      to the Most Vulnerable Citizens," *Boston
                      Review*, May 4, 2009.

Teresa Watanabe   "Helped During Misfortune, World War II
                      Internees Now Help Others," *Los Angeles Times*,
                      June 6, 2009.

Sherri Williams   "Uncommon Ground: Across the Country,
                      Africans and African-Americans Still Struggle
                      to Come Together," *Ebony*, July 2008.

Walter Williams   "A Nation of Cowards," Creators Syndicate,
                      Inc., February 25, 2009.

OPPOSING
VIEWPOINTS®
SERIES

CHAPTER 3

How Does Government Affect Race Relations?

Chapter Preface

In America, voluntary ethnic communities and legally en-forced segregation have proliferated since the Civil War, from small all-black towns in the South, to urban housing projects serving the predominantly minority poor, and local housing ordinances that prevented white home owners from selling their property to black buyers under threat of "prop-erty damage" lawsuits by white neighbors who end up living next door. Civil rights activism removed most of the laws per-petuating residential segregation by the 1960s, but banks and housing lenders practiced unofficial, often unintentional "mortgage discrimination" until the federal government took action in 1977 with the Community Reinvestment Act (CRA).

Requiring banks by law to serve members of all social and economic statuses or face business sanctions, the CRA and like legislation was intended to reduce the imbalance between whites and minority group members' ability to secure credit and purchase a home. Further legislation in 1980—the De-pository Institutions Deregulation and Monetary Control Act—made it easier for lenders to accommodate borrowers with lower monthly income, less money saved for a down payment, and weaker credit histories. Within a few years, the ability to purchase a home in safer residential communities with better schools was put into the hands of many thousands of minority group members who had been barred from this privilege, by active discrimination or circumstance, for genera-tions.

When the housing market and job economy is good, home ownership is a powerful tool for upward mobility. In addition to the freedom to choose where you want your children to live and go to school, a mortgage—even a high-risk one—is historically a safe financial investment. For several years, the racial homeownership gap narrowed and the color of the historically white suburbs changed. From this vantage point, government interference in the mortgage business had a positive, equalizing effect.

But when the economy is bad, high-risk mortgages—held disproportionately by the poor and minority groups—are a crushing liability. When the terms of these high-risk mortgages started increasing loan interest rates, monthly payments ballooned in size. With the recession of the late-2000s, fewer people sought to buy houses and the value of a house decreased significantly; homeowners struggling to keep up with payments could no longer sell their home in hopes of renting cheaper elsewhere, and ended up defaulting on loans. "Subprime Mortgages, Foreclosures, and Urban Neighborhoods," a study published by Federal Reserve economists Kristopher Gerardi and Paul Willen in 2008, reveals that black homeowners are foreclosed upon 50 percent more often than Hispanics and more than twice as often as whites. Furthermore, Rory Van Loo reveals in his 2009 *Albany Law Review* paper, "A Tale of Two Debtors: Bankruptcy Disparities by Race," that minorities who do file for bankruptcy are 40 percent less likely than whites to see relief. Minority homeowners who default on a risky loan often find themselves a few years later with no savings, no home, and terrible credit, generally much worse off than they were before buying a home. From this point of view, government interference in banks' lending practices in order to remedy racial disparities in homeownership has harmed minorities, and made people less financially secure than they would have been as renters.

Because government is complex and far-reaching, and because change happens over time, it is almost impossible to determine in advance whether laws and regulations intended to reduce racism and balance inequity will actually do so, which the housing boom and bust has demonstrated. The following chapter addresses some of the ways federal and local governments have attempted to counteract racism and whether these efforts achieved the desired effects.

> *"Relative to population, blacks have been arrested on drug charges at consistently higher rates than whites."*

Police Use Racial Profiling in the War on Drugs

Jamie Fellner

Jamie Fellner specializes in U.S. criminal justice issues, including prison conditions, the incarceration of the mentally ill, sentencing, the death penalty, and drug law enforcement. From 2001 to 2007, she was the first director of Human Rights Watch's U.S. program, supervising research and advocacy on U.S. counterterrorism policies, immigration, and the criminal justice system. The following viewpoint argues that the American "war on drugs" has put a disproportionate number of black Americans into prison, and claims that the racial imbalance of punishments for drug crimes is the result of racial profiling by local police organizations.

As you read, consider the following questions:

1. According to Fellner, what percent of drug arrestees in Seattle, Wash., are black?

Jamie Fellner, "Race, Drugs, and Law Enforcement in the United States," *Stanford Law & Policy Review*, vol. 20, 2009, pp. 257–274. Copyright © 2009 Stanford Law and Policy Review. Reproduced by permission.

2. According to the author, why is the race of the people in the upper echelons of the drug trade irrelevant to this analysis of drug arrests?

3. According to Police Commissioner Lee Brown, why do police officers target low-income neighborhoods (which are usually minority neighborhoods) for drug arrests?

Since the mid-1980s, the United States has pursued aggressive law enforcement strategies to curtail the use and distribution of illegal drugs. The costs and benefits of this national "war on drugs" remain fiercely debated. What is not debatable, however, is that this ostensibly race-neutral effort has been waged primarily against black Americans. Relative to their numbers in the general population and among drug offenders, black Americans are disproportionately arrested, convicted, and incarcerated on drug charges.

Public officials have been relatively untroubled by the disproportionate arrest and incarceration of blacks for drug offenses. Their relative indifference—and and that of the public at large—no doubt reflects, to varying degrees, partisan politics, "tough on crime" punitive philosophies, misinformation about drugs, an uncritical embrace of drug war logic, and misguided notions about the needs of poor urban communities. But to some extent it also reflects conscious and unconscious views about race. Indeed, those views have been woven into the very fabric of American anti-drug efforts, influencing the definition of the "drug problem" and the nature of the response to it.

Although whites are relatively untouched by anti-drug efforts compared to blacks, supporters of the drug war may not see a problem of race discrimination because they do not believe the purpose of drug law enforcement is to harm blacks—if anything, drug law enforcement is seen as protecting minority communities from addiction, harassment, and violence. Perhaps without realizing it, they have accepted the same definition of discrimination that the courts use in constitutional equal protection cases—absent ill-intent, there is no discrimination. . . .

Race Defines the Problem

Race has been and remains inextricably involved in drug law enforcement, shaping the public perception of and response to the drug problem. A recent study in Seattle [Wash.] is illustrative. Although the majority of those who shared, sold, or transferred serious drugs in Seattle are white (indeed seventy percent of the general Seattle population is white), almost two-thirds (64.2%) of drug arrestees are black. The racially disproportionate drug arrests result from the police department's emphasis on the outdoor drug market in the racially diverse downtown area of the city, its lack of attention to other outdoor markets that are predominantly white, and its emphasis on crack. Three-quarters of the drug arrests were crack-related even though only an estimated one-third of the city's drug transactions involved crack. Whites constitute the majority of those who deliver methamphetamine, ecstasy, powder cocaine, and heroin in Seattle; blacks are the majority of those who deliver crack. Not surprisingly then, seventy-nine percent of those arrested on crack charges were black. The researchers could not find a "racially neutral" explanation for the police prioritization of the downtown drug markets and crack. The focus on crack offenders, for example, did not appear to be a function of the frequency of crack transactions compared to other drugs, public safety or public health concerns, crime rates, or citizen complaints. . . .

The racial dynamics reflected in Seattle's current drug law enforcement priorities are long-standing and can be found across the country. Indeed, they provided the impetus for the "war on drugs" that began in the mid-1980s. Spearheaded by federal drug policy initiatives that significantly increased federal penalties for drug offenses and markedly increased federal funds for state anti-drug efforts, the drug war reflected the popularity of "tough on crime" policies emphasizing harsh punishment as the key to curbing drugs and restoring law and order in America. The drug of principal concern was crack cocaine, erroneously believed to be a drug used primarily by black Americans. . . .

Crack was the latest in a series of drugs that since the late nineteenth century have preoccupied policy makers in the United States. In each case, [according to researcher David Musto] "the drug of primary concern was strongly associated in the white public mind with a particular racial minority." Race was the lens through which drug problems in the United States were viewed, coloring both the definition of the problem and the proposed solutions. As the case of Seattle exemplifies, race continues today to influence the perceptions of the danger posed by those who use and sell illicit drugs, the choice of drugs that warrant the most public attention, and the choice of communities in which to concentrate drug law enforcement resources. . . .

Who Engages in Drug Offenses?

When asked to close their eyes and envision a drug offender, Americans did not picture a white middle class man snorting powder cocaine or college students smoking marijuana. They pictured unkempt African-American men and women slouched in alleyways or young blacks hanging around urban street corners. At least for the last twenty years, however, whites have engaged in drug offenses at rates higher than blacks.

According to the 2006 surveys conducted by the federal Substance Abuse and Mental Health Services Administration (SAMHSA), an estimated 49% of whites and 42.9% of blacks age twelve or older have used illicit drugs in their lifetimes: 14.5% of whites and 16% of blacks have used them in the past year: and 8.5% of whites and 9.8% of blacks have used

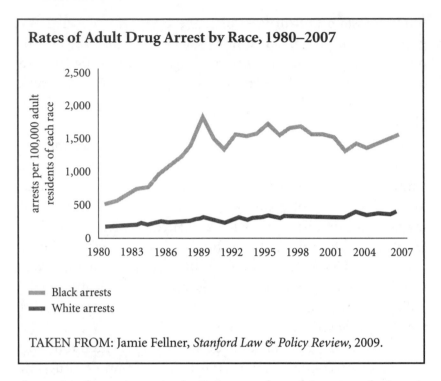

Rates of Adult Drug Arrest by Race, 1980–2007

arrests per 100,000 adult residents of each race

Black arrests
White arrests

TAKEN FROM: Jamie Fellner, *Stanford Law & Policy Review*, 2009.

them in the past month. Because the white population is more than six times greater than the black population, the absolute number of white drug offenders is far greater than that of black drug offenders. SAMHSA estimates that 111,774,000 people in the United States age twelve or older have used illicit drugs during their lifetime of whom 82,587,000 are white and 12,477,000 are black. Even among powder and crack cocaine users—which remain a principal focus of law enforcement there are more whites than blacks. According to SAMHSA's calculations, there are 27,083,000 whites who have used cocaine during their lifetime, compared to 2,618,000 blacks and, indeed, 5,553,000 whites who have used crack cocaine, compared to 1,537,000 blacks. . . .

Evidence regarding the race of drug sellers also emerges from research in specific urban drug markets. For example, the study of Seattle's drug market, discussed above, indicates that the majority of the drug sellers are white (as are a majority of the users). In fact, research suggests that drug users tend to obtain their drugs from people of the same race as themselves. . . .

Some might question whether blacks constitute a higher percentage than whites of persons occupying higher ranks in the drug business, e.g. major traffickers. Empirical research addressing this question is not available, but experts suggest that higher positions in the drug trade are not likely to be held by black individuals. The race of persons in the upper echelons of the drug trade is also not particularly relevant, because the overwhelming preponderance of drug offenders entering the criminal justice system are low-level non-violent offenders. For example, between 1980 and the present, arrests for drug sales, possession with intent to sell, manufacturing, transportation, or importing have never constituted more than 36% of all drug arrests. Drug offenders who are incarcerated are mostly street-level dealers, couriers, and other bit players in the drug trade.

Arrests and Incarceration of Drug Offenders

All other things being equal, if blacks constitute an estimated 13% to 20% of the total of black and white drug offenders, they, should constitute a roughly similar proportion of the total number of blacks and whites who are arrested, convicted, and sent to prison for drug law violations. But all other things are not equal. The data demonstrate clearly and consistently that blacks have been and remain more likely to be arrested for drug offending behavior relative to their percentage among drug offenders than whites who engage in the same behavior. There are many reasons for the racial disparities in drug arrests, including demographics, the extent of community complaints, police allocation of resources, racial profiling, and the relative case of making drug arrests in minority urban areas compared to white areas. One analyst [William J. Stuntz] has observed that in the war on drugs:

> Racial profiling is almost inevitable. Race becomes one of the readily observable visual clues to help identify drug suspects, along with age, gender and location. There is a certain rationality to this—if you are in poor black neighborhoods, drug dealers are more likely to be black. Local distribution networks are often monoracial; downscale markets are often neighborhood-based; and downscale urban neighborhoods are often segregated. . . . The law and practice of drug enforcement is market-specific, and the markets are divided by race and class.

Former New York Police Commissioner Lee Brown explained the police concentration in certain neighborhoods and the consequent racial impact as follows:

> In most large cities, the police focus their attention on where they see conspicuous drug use—street-corner drug sales— and where they get the most complaints. Conspicuous drug use is generally in your low-income neighborhoods that generally turn out to be your minority neighborhoods. . . . It's easier for police to make an arrest when you have people selling drugs on the street corner than those who are [selling or buying drugs] in the suburbs or in office buildings. The end result is that more blacks are arrested than whites because of the relative ease in making those arrests.

Between 1980 and 2007, there were more than twenty-five million adult drug arrests in the United States. The percentage of arrests that involved black men and women increased from 27% in 1980 to a high ranging from 40% to 42% between 1989 and 1993, and then declined more or less steadily to the current percentage of 35%. Relative to population, blacks have been arrested on drug charges at consistently higher rates than whites. In 1980 blacks were arrested at rates almost three (2.9) times the rate of whites. In the years with the worst disparities, between 1988 and 1993, blacks were arrested at rates more than five times the rate of whites. In the last six years, the ratio of black to white drug arrest rates has ranged between 3.5 and 3.9.

Although the ratio of black to white arrests has decreased somewhat since the mid 1990s when it was at its highest, racial disparity in drug arrests has continued despite changes in drug use and law enforcement priorities. . . . Methamphetamine manufacture and use emerged as law enforcement concerns in the late 1990s. Yet although marijuana use is prevalent across races, and methamphetamine is used primarily by whites, blacks continue to be disproportionately arrested.

The difference between the black proportion of drug offenders and the black proportion of drug arrests reflects the ongoing salience of urban drug law enforcement, or, more specifically, drug law enforcement in black urban neighborhoods. In 2007, for example, 77% of drug arrests occurred in cities. Although urban blacks account for approximately 6% of the national population, they constituted 29.8% of all drug arrests in 2007. A longitudinal analysis of urban drug arrests by race shows that in the largest American cities, drug arrests for African Americans rose at three times the rate for whites between 1980 and 2003, 225% compared to 70%. In eleven cities, black drug arrests rose by more than 500%. In the seventy-five largest counties in the United States, blacks in 2002 accounted for 46% of drug offense arrests, even though they represented only 15.6% of the population. New York State provides a particularly striking example: blacks in New York City represent 10.7% of the state population, yet accounted for 42.1% of drug arrests statewide.

"Race is but one component taken into consideration as police piece together various features comprising a 'scene' to determine whether it is sufficiently unusual to merit their intervention."

Police Do Not Consciously Use Racial Profiling

Vic Satzewich and William Shaffir

Vic Satzewich is a professor in the Sociology Department of McMaster University in Canada; his research interests include international migration, racism, and aboriginal/non-aboriginal relations in Canada. William Shaffir is a professor in the Sociology Department at the same institution. *The following viewpoint provides a background for police use of "racial profiling," and delves into some of the ways that police profile targets of suspicion. Although police officers admit that they do consider a suspect's race, they maintain that it is just one tool for assessing the likelihood of guilt. The authors find that police officers disagree that racism contributes to profiling's prevalence.*

Vic Satzewich and William Shaffir, "Racism vs. Professionalism: Claims and Counter-Claims about Racial Profiling," *Canadian Journal of Criminology and Criminal Justice*, vol. 51, April 2009, pp. 200–220. Copyright © 2009 Canadian Criminal Justice Association www.ccja-acjp.ca/en. Reproduced by permission of University of Toronto Press Inc. www.utpjournals.com.

As you read, consider the following questions:

1. According to the viewpoint, what outdoor activity does one officer compare profiling to?

2. What color are all police in uniform considered, according to one officer?

3. What, according to the authors, is the deflection strategy of blaming the victim?

Generally speaking, police chiefs, police union representatives, and police boards deny that racial profiling is practised in this country [Canada]. These denials are explained either as a form of *democratic racism* or, from the vantage point of [sociologist] Howard S. Becker's (1967) *hierarchy of credibility*, as outright lies told by those in power in order to protect their prestige and authority. In this paper, we want to suggest an alternative perspective on the issue of racial profiling.

Rather than interpreting police denials of racial profiling as a form of democratic racism, or as lies, this paper suggests that the concept of a police subculture offers the most credible backdrop for understanding what is commonly termed *racial profiling*. When contextualized in this manner, racial profiling is perceived by the police as one in a series of activities that define their work. We argue that, when seen in the context of police subcultures, such profiling occurs even in the absence of officers who may be inclined to prejudice or discrimination against members of visible minorities. As well, that subculture provides police with a powerful and convincing deflection rhetoric to neutralize claims that the policing institution has failed to root out the racist practices of its officers. Indeed, as our data based on interviews with police officers suggest, police officials feel confident that the organization's efforts to embrace diversity are to be applauded and that its critics should be condemned. . . .

Police Work Requires Profiling

From the perspective of the police with whom we met, police work necessarily involves attentiveness to particular signals and "unusual fits." It is precisely in this regard that profiling occupies centre stage in accomplishing police work. It is not difficult to appreciate how behaviour defined as racial profiling by police critics is otherwise defined as criminal profiling and professional conduct by members of the Hamilton Police Service [in Ontario, Canada]. In the following passage, a high-ranking officer emphasizes the importance of context for how police organize their activities and points out that, by failing to appreciate the total dynamics of police work, one can mistakenly conclude that blacks are singled out for differential treatment:

> I wouldn't be surprised if they did that [profiling]. Now, mind you, I don't work in the Jane–Finch area. I mean ask anybody about Jane–Finch and, all of a sudden, they begin to shudder . . . I know that because that's a reputation that has spread right across the map of Ontario . . . assaults, muggings, shootings, drugs, stabbings . . . they're all happening in Jane and Finch. So let's just pretend that that population there is mostly a black or immigrant population, . . . certainly not typical white. And if that's where the crime is, I'm going to be pulling over people who do crime. It's like going fishing. You go where the fish are if you're going to catch fish. If you're going to catch criminals, you end up having to do that . . .

A veteran of the services, himself a member of an ethnic minority, makes a similar point. Following specialized training, police work depends on profiling, but not the kind that is specifically linked to any particular race or culture:

> As police officers, we are trained in certain ways, and then you build instincts. Because when we're out on the street, we rely on our instincts. We are trained investigators in the

sense that we need to do profiling. And what kind of profiling is that? Criminal profiling. It has nothing to do with racial profiling ... We profile criminals. We do geographic profiling. It assists us to identify our problems and localize them and address them. When we go out ... we do not target any specific culture or race. However, if we do come into a problematic area, and we start to ply our trade—policing—then if they happen to fall within those parameters, there's not much we can do.

Another black officer sensitive to the claims made by critics of the police that racial profiling is endemic to policing underscores the necessity of distinguishing between profiling, in general, and racial profiling more specifically:

We talk about racial profiling in our office, and with our officers, and we say to a certain extent profiling exists in policing and you need it to some extent, but you have to recognize you can't label everyone, you know. You can say that I find stolen autos on the east mountain, for example, OK, so are you saying that all people that live on the east mountain steal cars? That's not a realistic a + b = c knowledge ... If I want to go look for stolen cars, ya, I might go look toward the east mountain. But it doesn't mean that's always the case and all people on the east mountain steal cars ... A certain amount of profiling does exist in policing. It has to exist.

More generally, however, police situate profiling within the broader context of police work that can only be appreciated at a distance by the larger public. Referring to the responsibilities faced by the police, a minority officer reflects:

It's a very difficult job, and the nature of the job forces you to stereotype and discriminate. When I'm driving my cruiser at 2 o'clock in the morning, and I see ... [one of the interviewers] in a shirt and tie driving a Mercedes, I think nothing of it. But if I was to see a black twenty-year-old, guess what? He's getting pulled over.

Rationalizing the Use of Profiling

The following excerpt emphasizes that race is but one component taken into consideration as police piece together various features comprising a "scene" to determine whether it is sufficiently unusual to merit their intervention:

> Some people seem to think that race is a dominating factor in the way the police do their job; that is, there's a black guy walking down the street. I'm going to stop him, maybe he's a drug dealer or something. [Right.] Whereas race is really one of several factors that the police will look at. Like, for instance, you might see a black guy walking down the street. He might be wearing a certain style of clothes, baggy clothes, hip-hop type clothes. [Right.] He might have a red bandana which is often worn by gang members. He might meet up with another guy. You might see them kind of make a hand slide to each other . . . You might see the one guy reach out, they quickly exchange something hand-to-hand. You look at all those factors. The conclusion the police officer is going to come to is a drug deal just went down. Looking at all those factors employed, the hand-to-hand, the hand slides, but when you approach that person, well [he will claim], they're just busting my ass cause I'm black.

In addition to offering a lens through which to view the unique challenges of their work, the occupational culture enables the police to draw upon a vocabulary of explanations . . . called *motives*. This vocabulary is composed of a series of rationalizations and accounts police (in this instance) use to explain their situation to themselves and others. Many such police rationalizations permit them to deny responsibility when faced with the allegation that their profiling is racially motivated. This type of rationalization . . . offers a more credible explanation than race-driven motives—one that more accurately reflects practical considerations and provides them with a way of viewing their own actions as "normal," in line with what would be expected of them. Such tactics, then, not only explain an event but also enable officers to save face by deflecting possible feelings of guilt or shame in connection with their interactions with minorities. In their analysis of the accounts employed by defeated politicians to manage the stigma of defeat and to cope with the repercussions of loss, [researchers William] Shaffir and [Steven] Kleinknecht refer to such coping mechanisms as *deflection rhetoric*, a term that suits our purpose in understanding how the police attend to the charges against them of being racially motivated. . . .

Blaming the Victim

Yet a different deflection strategy used by police to explain away allegations of racial profiling involves turning the tables and suggesting that, if there is a problem, the problem lies elsewhere, particularly in the individuals and organizations who claim that racial profiling is a problem.

As a number of other students of police subcultures have noted, the police subculture is characterized by a "we"/"they" mentality. The construction of non-police as others is augmented by the belief that it is the other that holds racist attitudes towards the police. Both of these themes were evident in the following explanation by one black officer of how the police are the true victims of racism:

> When you get a call and you're a black person or a white person, Vietnamese or whatever you are, you get called a pig just the same, you know? You might get called something else pig, in front of that or whatever, but you get that from different groups of people. Like black people have called me that . . . So depending what they think what type of nationality you are, they call you that, people in the community; but they're upset, tensions are high—but I think when we all put the uniform on, we're all looked at like police officers.

This officer went on to explain, "[W]hen you put on the uniform, you're all blue."

Several officers, both black and white, recounted specific situations where individuals of minority backgrounds played the so-called "race card" against the police to deflect attention away from their own wrong-doing. As one female Aboriginal officer told us:

> I remember one specific incident and I stopped the person like 250 metres away. I can't see who's driving 250 metres away. I can see the car . . . The driver's black, [and] right off the bat starts off, "[Y]ou stopped me because I was black." I said, "[W]hat? From 250 metres away, I couldn't see if you were pink from 250 metres away." . . .

Some officers claim that individuals who make allegations of racial profiling, or who believe that racial profiling is widespread, are simply invoking the Rodney King incident in Los Angeles [in 1991]. As one black officer explained:

> Again, the kinds of people that you're dealing with, when you're dealing with the criminal who happens to be an ethnic minority, they may throw race at you. And it's not that police are racist, it's just the nature of our job that you have to deal with people in a certain way, and it comes across that way. I mean, if a black guy breaks into a house and comes running out, and there's three white police officers there, and that black guy doesn't wanna go to jail, he's gonna fight his way to get free no matter what. People who are gonna watch this only are gonna be thinking of one thing—of Rodney King, and look at these racist cops, beating up this black guy. Meanwhile, if it was a white guy and this white guy decides he's not going to jail and he's gonna fight no matter what, the same thing's gonna happen.

Clearly, the deflection strategy of blaming the victim, where the police are portrayed as the true victims of racism, is to attribute allegations of racial profiling to the uninformed and misinformed public who have little direct experience of policing or police work. . . .

Police Do Not Realize That They Racially Profile

It is important to know whether discrimination and social exclusion are driven by intentions and by beliefs that certain groups of people are inferior to others or whether discrimination is the unintentional outcome of taken-for-granted processes followed by, or decisions made by, individuals who do not hold beliefs about the superiority or inferiority of certain groups of people. In other words, if we want to seek an appropriate solution to the problem of racial profiling, we need to have a clear assessment of the source of the problem.

A key to unravelling the puzzle of the police force's reliance on racial profiling ties this issue to professionalism and police work. Policing, maintain the police, requires a level of conduct that cannot be undermined by concerns that minorities, or any interest group for that matter, may cry foul or be identified as victims of unfair targeting. From the perspective of the police, while particular groups may garner attention, this is hardly the outcome of racialized police practices; they engage in criminal profiling, not racial profiling.

> *"An insufficient number of bilingual officers can cause trauma to crime victims ... and endangers officers who cannot immediately communicate with criminal suspects."*

Police Departments Should Be Multilingual

James Pinkerton and Meg Loucks

James Pinkerton writes for The Houston Chronicle *and other news organizations, and worked in the administrations of Ronald Reagan and George H.W. Bush. Meg Loucks is the media manager at* The Houston Chronicle; *she has won journalism awards for her videography. The following viewpoint reveals Houston, Texas, as a city where foreign languages (about one hundred) are spoken among nearly half its population. Although the Houston Police Department provides many language support services and financial incentives for officers to become bilingual, the authors report that many crime victims and witnesses find themselves unable to communicate with the police who first arrive on the scene.*

As you read, consider the following questions:

1. According to the authors, what percentage of the Houston police force is bilingual?

2. In addition to Spanish, bilingual officers are also needed for what two South Asian languages, according to the authors?

3. Why, according to Pinkerton and Loucks, does Houston resident Nancy Moreno feel desperate about speaking with police who speak only English?

Police officers arriving at a murder scene at a north side apartment complex could not speak Spanish to the residents, so a cameraman from a local TV station translated until bilingual officers arrived hours later.

It is a situation that plays out across Houston [Texas] several times a week as officers who speak only English rely on wrecker [tow truck] drivers, bystanders or victims' children to act as translators if bilingual officers are not available.

Despite a Houston Police Department [HPD] program that pays $1.9 million annually in extra pay to 1,046 bilingual-certified officers—nearly 20 percent of the 5,300-officer force—there are frequent situations when officers cannot speak with the residents they serve, officers say. Of those, 904 officers are certified as fluent in Spanish. Other certifications include officers who can speak Vietnamese, two dialects of Chinese and Korean.

The issue of language fluency is crucial in Houston, an international city that long has been a magnet for immigrants from around the world. For example, the Houston Independent School District has identified about 100 languages spoken in students' homes, a district spokesman said.

Language Barriers Further Hurt Victims

Critics say an insufficient number of bilingual officers can cause trauma to crime victims, burdens the bilingual officers with greater case loads, and endangers officers who cannot immediately communicate with criminal suspects.

The lack of bilingual officers often forces victims to recount the intimate details of a sexual attack to a neighbor acting as a translator for an officer, said one veteran HPD investigator, adding he encountered the situation several times a month.

"On a homicide case when you have to go to an outsider—not an officer, not a detective, not an investigator—to use them to translate or interpret, that's bad enough," said the officer, who asked not to be identified because he had not been authorized to speak to the news media. "But if you could imagine a family violence case, a sexual assault case, or where a juvenile has been assaulted, and having to use a neighbor, or a family member, or someone off the street to tell about something that real intimate, personal, private—it's horrible. It's a second victimization."

The officer said because of the high number of Hispanic victims, the four bilingual officers in his 24-investigator juvenile sex crimes unit had caseloads that were up to four times as high as officers who spoke only English.

Rosalinda Ybanez, a Houston police officer who is president of the Organization of Spanish Speaking Officers, said HPD does not have enough Spanish-speaking officers in a city where the population is estimated to be 42 percent Hispanic.

"The reason is because it seems that the chief has not ever actually paid attention to the problem of servicing the Hispanic community, and especially the Hispanic community that speaks Spanish only," Ybanez said.

Are Police Meeting the Needs of the Community?

Former Houston Police Chief Harold Hurtt, in an interview shortly before he retired Dec. 31, [2009] said HPD has enough bilingual officers to meet the city's needs. When victims can-

The Languages of Houston's Residents and Police

A little more than 19 percent of HPD officers speak a language other than English. Of those, 86 percent speak Spanish.

Non-Bilingual Officers: 80.4%
Bilingual Officers: 19.6%
Total: 5,323

Languages Spoken by Bilingual Officers
Spanish: 904 (86.4%)
Vietnamese: 111 (10.6%)
Korean: 11 (1.05%)
Cantonese: 11 (1.05%)
Mandarin: 9 (0.8%)

Houston's Ethnic Composition
Asian: 5.3%
Hispanic: 42%
All Other: 52.7%

Data from: U.S. Census Bureau, HPD

TAKEN FROM: Alberto Cuadra, "Bilingual Police," *Houston Chronicle*, January 10, 2010.

not communicate with officers, they can call a telephone translation service, he said, adding that Hispanic officers are assigned to every division of the department.

"But when we hire a police officer in Houston, we hire them to serve the community, not one element of the population," Hurtt said. "You try to train them and equip them so they can do that. I would just hate to hire a specific group of officers. Let's say they didn't have the same size workload as the others had, or a greater work load than the others; it wouldn't be fair. So I think we equal out the work assignments in the organization, and we meet the needs of all of our victims."

HPD used to have a "Chicano Squad" in homicide and several other divisions composed of Hispanic officers, but they were dismantled during Hurtt's tenure. Only the Latino Squad in the robbery division and an Asian gang squad remain. Today, the eight bilingual investigators, two sergeants and a lieutenant in the Latino robbery squad handle 40 percent of the robberies in the city, said Robbery Squad Sgt. [Sergeant] Edward Diaz.

"A week doesn't go by that someone from another division calls ours for help with a translation or a victim's statement," Diaz said.

The need for bilingual officers is not exclusive to the Spanish-speaking community. Houston has thousands of Indian immigrants whose native language is Hindi, as well as a large Pakistani population whose members speak Urdu, noted immigration lawyer Gordon Quan.

"It certainly seems we have a growing south Asian population, many who speak Urdu and Hindi, and it's important because we have a lot of grocers and other businesspeople who are more comfortable in those languages," said Quan, a former City Council member. "I think it would be reasonable to expand it."

Quan said bilingual officers should be assigned to areas of the city where they are accessible to different ethnic communities.

Miscommunication Can Be Dangerous

This summer, Nancy Moreno, 21, and her husband awoke to hear a struggle outside their north side apartment, and soon learned their neighbor had been gunned down on the sidewalk. Her husband could not speak to the officers who first arrived on the scene, and identified their slain neighbor to the police with the help of a Spanish-speaking journalist.

Hours later, bilingual officers arrived, and several days later police arrested two men and charged them with murder.

The inability to speak with police officers when an emergency arises "makes me feel desperate," Moreno said. "I'm a mother who is almost always alone with my child. Having to report something . . . you don't feel confident because you're not going to be understood."

The situation is the reverse for patrol officer Casey Lewis, a non-Spanish speaker who works on the city's east side, where most of the residents are Hispanic. He acknowledged having to use pedestrians or wrecker drivers, even the young children of victims, to translate for him if bilingual officers are not available to assist.

"It would definitely benefit me if I was in a situation where I was being understood by everyone I was encountering out here," the officer said during a recent patrol. "But, yeah, it makes it a little more dangerous. . . . I don't know what they are saying, and they don't know what I am saying. Lack of communication is not good . . . especially when you're dealing with people who have guns, knives."

> *"Residents of this or any nation should learn the language of that nation if they intend to function in that society. It is just that simple."*

The Government Should Conduct Its Business in English Only

Beaufort Observer

The Beaufort Observer *is an online publication for the community of Beaufort County in North Carolina. It focuses on local news and matters of interest, and addresses current topics from a variety of political perspectives. The following viewpoint first appeared as an editorial on a controversy over the publication of certain state government Web site pages in Spanish. It argues that the people and governments of the United States should use a single common language—English—and that translating government documents into foreign languages prevents immigrants from assimilating to American culture and marginalizes them as second-class citizens.*

Beaufort Observer, "What's Wrong with Spanish on the State Websites?" February 15, 2010. Reproduced by permission.

As you read, consider the following questions:

1. What are two symbols of the American "melting pot," as suggested by the author?

2. Why does the viewpoint author make the case that immigrants are insulted if the government does not require them to learn to read and write English?

3. Why does the author contend that Spanish Web pages are irrelevant?

Governor [of North Carolina] Beverly Perdue just does not "get it." Or, at least the staff person who answers her mail doesn't.

The Beaufort County [N.C.] Commission recently voted to ask the Governor to explain why state websites are posted in Spanish and requesting that Spanish be removed from all state websites. The action is one in a series that the County Commission, led by Hood Richardson, Stan Deatherage and Al Klemm have taken in recent months related to the issue of bilingualism impacting Beaufort County.

The Governor's response was essentially: "People who read only Spanish need the information our websites furnish and therefore we're going to continue to provide that." (We'll dispense here with the absurdity of her reasoning of trying to use Spanish to promote tourism, but we'll show in a moment why it is an absolutely specious [plausible, but false] argument. And whoever wrote Perdue's response certainly should know that.) . . .

We think the issue of bilingualism is one of the most significant issues this nation faces right now and by logical extension it becomes one of the most significant issues the State of North Carolina and the County of Beaufort face. Here's why.

"Melting Pot" vs. "Balkanization"

For most of its history America has been what has euphemistically been referred to as a "Melting Pot." Most of us are descendants of immigrants, either forced or willing. American literature and history is filled with stories of immigrants who came to this country and "made good." And indeed, we would contend that immigration has been one of the bedrock strengths upon which this nation has prospered, and therefore we are all better off because of immigration.

But the history of immigration in America has been one of cultural assimilation. Immigrants who came here assimilated into the American culture and the American culture evolved as a result of the Melting Pot phenomenon. And we think that is good. In fact, we would go so far as to suggest it is a truly and uniquely American tradition as symbolized by the Statue of Liberty and Ellis Island. Even in our Pledge of Allegiance we say ". . . one nation . . ."

But these times are different. The current trend in immigration, specifically and particularly related to Hispanic immigrants, is not assimilation but one of separateness. Under the liberal guise of "diversity" and "multi-culturalism" we as a culture have gravitated toward a de facto national policy of Balkanization [a phenomenon in which the people of a nation splinter into ethnic alliances].

You have to have a pretty deep background in history to fully understand the implications of Balkanization and space does not permit a discussion of the concept here except to suggest that it is a fundamental issue that should be addressed with significant seriousness by our leaders . . . at all levels. Governor Perdue's letter, if nothing else, would indicate that she has a rather flimsy understanding of that issue. . . .

We don't think there should be any question that assimilation is a preferable public policy to Balkanization. It seems so obvious to us.

Accommodating Spanish Speakers Is Condescending

We think putting Spanish signs up in county offices, having "push 1 for English, push 2 for Spanish" on answering systems, sending home notices in Spanish via school children, holding Spanish-speaking meetings for parents, and offering Spanish on websites is ultimately condescending toward not only non-English speaking people but toward America as well. That is what Hood means when he says "it's unpatriotic." It is actually ignorance. Ignorance of what made this country great and ignorance of what an "educated citizenry" actually means. There is simply no excuse for educators to denigrate the value of language fluency. Educate non-English speaking people, don't relegate them to second class status.

Think about it. Suppose our education officials announced tomorrow that "we have decided that our students really don't need to learn to read and write, so we're dropping those courses from our curriculum." Surely all hell would break loose. Parents would protest and rightly so for depriving our children of the skills they need to be successful in life. And they would be right and it would be important enough that such educators should be banished from the profession. Yet that is exactly what we do when we by official action infer to non-English speaking people that it is not essential to learn English. We do them no favors whatsoever to accommodate bilingualism. We certainly should not accept illiteracy from a group of people because of their ethnic background. (You really have to ponder that to fully grasp the profound significance and implications of that idea.)

Liberals pacify themselves by thinking they are being kind and helpful to English illiterates (look it up) when they accommodate and even facilitate cultural bilingualism. But they are actually being despotic in the worst sort of way. They are relegating non-English speaking people to serfdom, just as surely as if we allowed our students to graduate without being able to read and write any language.

Monolingualism Is the Most Practical Answer

Residents of this or any nation should learn the language of that nation if they intend to function in that society. It is just that simple. "When in Rome do as the Romans do . . ." and all that. And if you logically can accept that concept then we get to the debate that we should be having . . . "which language constitutes literacy?"

But any reasonable person would make short order of that debate. It is simple, in any society: The language of commerce. And of that there is no real legitimate argument. In most of the world, not just in the United States, the language of commerce is English. (If you don't believe it, just check to see how the overwhelming majority of computers and networks function. Overwhelmingly, more binary code produces English characters than any other). Commerce is conducted primarily in English (and Chinese) and the other languages are translations . . . just as Governor Perdue does on her websites. Translation is not only inefficient, it is invidious discrimination against non-English speaking people.

And in relation to the website issue, as opposed to other facets of bilingualism, the Spanish webpages are completely irrelevant. Anyone with a basic knowledge of computers knows that you can translate any page or website from any language into any other language, except Southern, with a couple of mouse clicks. Thus, posting Spanish is nothing more than pandering for votes or smoke and mirrors but the "official message" it sends is far from innocuous.

The majority of our County Commission is correct on this issue. Our Governor is wrong. But she's a liberal, so what can you expect?

> "A black applicant [to the University of Michigan] was 71 times more likely to be admitted than a white with the same SAT score, high school grades, and background."

Affirmative Action Is Legalized Discrimination

Steven Farron

Steven Farron is a retired professor of Classics from the University of Witwatersrand in South Africa and the author of the book, The Affirmative Action Hoax. *The following viewpoint was written soon after Michigan banned affirmative action programs for school admissions and employment. Farron explains how the University of Michigan had implemented a scoring system for student applications that awarded more points for being black, Hispanic, or Native American than for scoring a perfect score on qualifying exams. White students with equivalent scores are far less likely to be admitted, Farron argues, even though they perform much better academically after enrolling.*

Steven Farron, "Why Michigan Needed to Ban Preferences," *American Renaissance*, vol. 18, January 2007. Reproduced by permission.

As you read, consider the following questions:

1. According to Farron, on what qualifications for admission were student applicants to the University of Michigan assessed, and how were these characteristics scored?

2. What was the majority opinion about the future need for affirmative action programs in the ruling on the *Grutter v. Bollinger* Supreme Court case?

3. According to the viewpoint author, what percent of black students admitted to the University of Michigan in 2004 later went on academic probation?

On November 7, [2006] the Michigan electorate voted 58 to 42 percent in favor of what came to be called "Proposal 2," which was, to quote its text, "A proposal to amend the state constitution to ban affirmative action programs that give preferential treatment to groups or individuals based on their race, gender, color, ethnicity or national origin for public employment, education or contracting purposes." Its intent was the same as that of the Civil Rights Act of 1964: to guarantee equal treatment. Like the voters of California who passed a similar ban in 1996, and the voters of Washington State who did the same in 1998, the people of Michigan were, in effect, saying "and now we really mean it." . . .

On November 8, the day after the proposal passed, the president of the University of Michigan (U-M), Mary Sue Coleman, staggered to the microphone in a state of distress. In return for her annual salary of $742,148, the taxpayers of Michigan got the following statement: "I will not allow this university to go down the path of mediocrity. That is not Michigan. Diversity makes us strong, and it is too critical to our mission, too critical to our excellence, and too critical to our future to simply abandon."

"It's nothing personal, Osgood — We're letting you go as part of our affirmative action program."

© Rex May (baloo)/CartoonStock.com.

We shall see below the extent of the racial discrimination U-M practiced in order to prevent "mediocrity" and attain "diversity." It did so in the shelter of two widely publicized Supreme Court decisions.

Judicial Support of Affirmative Action

In June 2003, in *Gratz v. Bollinger*, the Supreme Court ruled that the method used by U-M's undergraduate College of Literature, Science and Arts at Ann Arbor to practice racial discrimination was unconstitutional. The university had been assigning applicants a certain number of points for various qualifications and characteristics, including race. For example, an outstanding essay earned a maximum of three points; being the child of an alumnus, four points; personal achieve-

117

ment, leadership, or public service, a maximum of five points; a perfect score on the SAT or ACT [standardized tests for college admission], 12 points; and *being black, Hispanic, or Native American 20 points*. The only other qualification worth 20 points was the difference between a 4.0 (i.e., straight As) high school GPA (grade point average) and a 3.0 (a B average). Socioeconomic background made no difference. The child of a black or Hispanic multimillionaire had an automatic 20 point advantage over the child of non-English-speaking Bulgarian immigrants.

The Supreme Court ruled that racial discrimination in admissions does not violate the Constitution, but the mechanical, numerical manner in which the undergraduate college implemented it does. On the same day, the Supreme Court ruled in *Grutter v. Bollinger* that the discrimination U-M's law school practiced, which was at least as great as that practiced by the undergraduate school, was being done in the correct, flexible, constitutional manner. As the justices put it, race was part of a "highly individualized, holistic review of each applicant's file," rather than the cold formula the undergraduate school used. However, the majority also stated:

> It would be a sad day indeed, were America to become a quota ridden society, with each identifiable minority assigned proportional representation in every desirable walk of life. But that is not the rationale for programs of preferential treatment; the acid test of their justification will be their efficacy in eliminating the need for any racial or ethnic preferences at all ... We expect that in twenty-five years from now, the use of racial preferences will no longer be necessary.

In their dissent from the majority in the *Gratz* decision, Justices Ruth Ginsburg and David Souter pointed out that rulings like these would simply encourage universities to discriminate with "winks, nods, and disguises," rather than openly and honestly. That, of course, is exactly what U-M proceeded to do, and the evidence now is available for all to see.

Unfair Admissions Policies

The Center for Equal Opportunity (CEO) and the Michigan Association of Scholars have obtained data on the admissions policies and academic performance of students in Michigan's undergraduate, law, and medical schools since the *Grutter* and *Gratz* decisions, and have published them on CEO's website.

The median combined verbal and math SAT scores of undergraduates admitted in 2005 was 1160 for blacks, 1260 for Hispanics, 1350 for whites, and 1400 for Asians (scores run from 400 to 1600). The median high school grade point average was 3.4 for blacks, 3.6 for Hispanics, 3.8 for Asians, and 3.9 for whites. A black or Hispanic in-state, male applicant with no alumni connection, a combined SAT score of 1240, and a 3.2 high school GPA had a 90 percent chance of being admitted. A white or Asian with the same record had a 10 percent chance.

This level of racial discrimination was considerably greater than before the *Gratz* and *Grutter* decisions, as shown by changes in what is called the odds ratio. This is the difference in chances of being admitted for applicants of different races with the same SAT or ACT score and high school GPA, controlling for in-state/out-of-state residence, sex, and alumni connections. In 2005, a black applicant was 71 times more likely to be admitted than a white with the same SAT score, high school grades, and background. For applicants who took the ACT, the odds ratio was 63 to one. The Hispanic-white odds ratios were 46 to one for the SAT and 48 to one for the ACT. For students admitted in 1999—before the Supreme Court decisions—the odds ratios were not so unfavorable to whites: The black-white odds ratio was 27 to one on the SAT, and 49 to one on the ACT; the Hispanic-white odds ratio was

12 to one on the SAT and 32 to one on the ACT. (To put these ratios into perspective, a smoker is 14 times more likely to die of lung cancer than a non-smoker.) The clear, numerical method of discrimination U-M used before the Supreme Court rulings held the admissions office in check; "flexible," "holistic" discrimination removed these restraints.

As always, discrimination in admissions is reflected in subsequent academic performance. . . .

The proportions of students admitted to U-M in 2004, who later went on academic probation were: blacks, 25 percent; Hispanics, 23 percent; Asians, 8 percent; whites, 5 percent. In this context, it is worth noting, as I explain in my book, *The Affirmative Action Hoax*, that blacks and Hispanics receive massive preferences in college grading, and take much easier courses than whites and Asians.

It is significant also that the academic performance of whites was better than that of Asians. That was also true of the two other years, 1999 and 2003, for which information on grades is available. Nevertheless, opponents of affirmative action at U-M and elsewhere have concentrated on its unfairness to Asians. In fact, whites are the greatest victims of affirmative action, but opponents claim that Asians are the main victims in order not to have to defend whites.

The main basis for the claim that Asians are the primary victims of affirmative action is that at most universities their average combined verbal and math SAT score is higher than that of whites. However, the combined score is misleading. Asians have a considerably higher average math score than whites, but a lower average verbal score. The math difference is greater than the verbal difference, but for most university subjects, the verbal test is a better indicator of academic performance. The white/Asian difference in average ACT scores for students admitted to U-M was negligible, and whites had higher average high school grades.

Graduate School Admissions Are Also Unfair

At U-M's law school, racial preferences did decline after the 2003 Supreme Court decisions, but were still enormous. A black who applied in 2005 was 18 times more likely to be admitted than a white or Asian with the same LSAT (Law School Admission Test) score, undergraduate GPA, residence status, sex, and alumni connections. A Hispanic was more than three times more likely to be admitted than a white or Asian.

In 2005, an in-state black male with no alumni connections had a 70 percent chance of admission if his LSAT score and undergraduate GPA were equal to the median of blacks who were admitted. A Hispanic with the same qualifications and background had a 30 percent chance of admission; a white or Asian had a 10 percent chance.

At U-M medical school, in 2005, the odds favoring a black or Hispanic applicant over a comparable white applicant were 21 to 1 and 5.5 to 1, respectively. . . .

Universities Insist on Discrimination

A warning: The legal abolition of racial discrimination in Michigan is not a cause for rejoicing but for heightened vigilance. Wherever racial discrimination has been banned, public universities have responded by adopting devious, circuitous, and deliberately confusing admissions criteria that make clear racial comparisons impossible. In 1996, U-M's president emeritus James Duderstadt said, "We will continue to do this [practice racial discrimination] until the Supreme Court says we can't any more . . . [Then] we'll try to find other ways to get the same result." After the vote, the current president, Mary Sue Coleman, vowed not to abandon racial discrimination. On the night before, she issued the following statement, "Regardless of what happens with Proposal 2, the University of Michigan will remain fully and completely committed to diversity. I am determined to do whatever it takes to sustain our excellence by recruiting and retaining a diverse community of students, faculty and staff."

> "It may be the ultimate expression of institutionalized racial bias that standardized test results, which provide proof to social scientists of bias against African Americans as a racial group, are used in our courts as the basis for proof of reverse discrimination against any member of the white race favored by the test results."

Affirmative Action Is Not Legalized Discrimination

Asa Gordon

Asa Gordon is secretary general of the Sons and Daughters of United States Colored Troops and executive director of the Douglass Institute of Government. In the following viewpoint, Gordon discusses Justice Clarence Thomas and his dissenting minority opinion in Grutter v. Bollinger, *in which the Supreme Court upheld the University of Michigan's affirmative action admissions policy. Through Gordon's critique of Justice Thomas, she explains why affirmative action admissions policies are both valuable and necessary, and why claims that these programs represent "reverse racism" are incorrect and unjustified.*

Asa Gordon, "A Color-blind Supreme Court?" *World & I*, 19.2, February 2004, pg. 38.

As you read, consider the following questions:

1. How does the message of Frederick Douglass relate to Justice Clarence Thomas and his dissenting minority in *Grutter v. Bollinger*?

2. What does Gordon use the sociology report "Measured Lies: The Bell Curve Examined" to illustrate?

3. How does the viewpoint define reverse racism?

Frederick Douglass, in response to a "color-blind" civil rights ruling by a conservative Supreme Court 121 years ago, delivered a message lost on Justice Clarence Thomas and his dissenting minority in *Grutter v. Bollinger*, decided June 23, 2003. "It is our lot to live among a people whose laws, traditions, and prejudices have been against us for centuries, and from these they are not yet free," observed Douglass. "To assume that they are free from these evils simply because they have changed their laws is to assume what is utterly unreasonable and contrary to facts. Large bodies move slowly. Individuals may be converted on the instant and change their whole course of life. Nations never. Time and events are required for the conversion of nations."

Douglass' poignant outburst proved to be a prophetic critique of the Supreme Court's assertion in 1883 that American society had arrived at a stage where it could treat its citizens with color-blind fairness, providing African Americans full equality with other citizens of the United States. In this emasculation of the amendments and acts that formed the foundation of Reconstruction, Justice Joseph P. Bradley's majority opinion declared: "When a man has emerged from slavery and by the aid of beneficent legislation has shaken off the inseparable concomitants of that state, there must be some stage in the progress of his elevation when he takes the rights of a mere citizen and ceases to be the special favorite of the law and when his rights as a citizen or a man are to be protected in the ordinary mode by which other men's rights are to be protected."

Thus the Supreme Court took the position that only 18 years removed from the constitutional amendment that abolished slavery, sufficient time had passed to sunset race-conscious "beneficent legislation" to redress the legacy of American slavery. In a chilling resurrection of this discredited reasoning, Justice Sandra Day O'Connor delivered the opinion of the Court in *Grutter v. Bollinger* that "25 years from now, the use of racial preferences will no longer be necessary to further the interest [in racial diversity] approved today."

In *Grutter*, the Court formally embraced the color-blind reasoning of Justice Lewis Powell in *Regents of the University of California v. Bakke* (1978) that sufficient time had passed since *Brown v. Board of Education* (1954) to justify sunsetting race-conscious, "beneficent" affirmative action polices to redress the legacy of American apartheid. Indeed, the Court announced its intention to fully embrace the rationale of Justice Bradley's 1883 opinion ending Reconstruction.

Naive Supreme Court

Douglass' observations on the naivete of the Supreme Court's color-blind reasoning in the civil rights cases (1883) are clearly lost on the majority of our contemporary Supreme Court justices. Douglass declared that "the practical construction of American life is a convention against us. Human law may know no distinction among men in respect of rights, but human practice may. Examples are painfully abundant."

Grutter provides a contemporary example of how standardized testing serves as a "practical construction of American life" that negates efforts to redress racial inequity. The mere allegation of reverse racism transforms proof of group bias by an oppressive group into proof of bias against a member of the oppressing group. It is a universal sociological axiom that statistically significant underachievement by any distinct group on standardized test scores is a manifest realization of that group's low ethnic status or position in the social structure that administers the test.

As sociologists report in "Measured Lies: The Bell Curve Examined," in Sweden, Finnish people are viewed as inferior.

Thus, "the failure rate for Finnish children in Swedish schools is very high. When Finnish children immigrate to Australia, however, they do well—as well as Swedish immigrants. Koreans do poorly in Japanese schools where they are viewed as culturally inferior; in American schools, on the other hand, Korean immigrants are very successful. The examples are numerous, but the results generally follow the same pattern: racial, ethnic, and class groups who are viewed negatively or as inferiors in a nation's dominant culture tend to perform poorly academically. Understood this way, groups' test scores are not the beginning of an explanation for inequality but the end of one. The beginning is history."

Not Reverse Racism

Therefore, it may be the ultimate expression of institutionalized racial bias that standardized test results, which provide proof to social scientists of bias against African Americans as a racial group, are used in our courts as the basis for proof of reverse discrimination against any member of the white race favored by the test results. Admissions policies are thus precluded from any consideration of race to redress test results that establish societal racism against blacks as a class to the detriment of individual whites.

This is the ironic nature of the evidential underpinning of American jurisprudence that is at the foundation of *Bakke, Hopwood, Taxman, and Gratz.* A charge of reverse racism by any individual white will ensure that this nation's forward drive in racial inequity for blacks will be fueled by a test engine that in fact proves blacks are victimized as a racial group by the dominant white culture.

Douglass, in his "Address to the People of the United States" (September 24, 1883), declared: "Though the colored man is no longer subject to be bought and sold, he is still surrounded by an adverse sentiment which fetters all his movements. In his downward course he meets with no resistance, but his course upward is resented and resisted at every step of his progress. . . . The color line meets him everywhere. . . . In spite of all your religion and laws he is a rejected man . . . and yet he is asked to forget his color, and forget that which everybody else remembers. . . . He is sternly met on the color line, and his claim to consideration in some way is disputed on the ground of color."

Thus in commentary made over 120 years ago, Douglass specifically addressed a Supreme Court ruling on civil rights legislation deemed by the Court to be "beneficent" to the black race and "disputed on the ground of color." That ruling precisely mirrors the current opinions on affirmative action held by Justice Thomas and his conservative colleagues on the Court. Douglass' comments are as devastating to today's conservative justices as they were one score and a century ago.

Selective Ignorance

In his dissenting opinion in *Grutter*, Justice Thomas chose to ignore contemporary remarks made by Douglass that were clearly relevant to the Supreme Court's disingenuous historical use of color-blind rationales in interpreting the equal protection clause of the Fourteenth Amendment. Instead, he selected remarks Douglass made before the Fourteenth Amendment was adopted into the Constitution.

The following extract is taken from Justice Thomas' deceptive editing of Douglass' 1865 address: "In regard to the colored people, there is always more that is benevolent, I per-

The Fiscal Benefits of Increasing Opportunity

Providing undocumented students access to higher education benefits the state [New Mexico] by increasing taxable income and decreasing social services payments. People who have college degrees have the potential to earn more than those who only have a high school diploma. Studies indicate that a bachelor's degree can lead to a yearly salary of almost twice that of someone with a high school diploma. In addition, academic success leads to reduced reliance on state expenditures such as health care, social services, and corrections.

Colleges and universities also benefit from granting in-state tuition to undocumented students. Some argue that granting in-state tuition to undocumented students causes universities to lose money that they otherwise could have collected. This argument is flawed because it presupposes that undocumented students will attend college even without qualifying for in-state tuition. . . . It is highly unlikely that undocumented students will go to college if they cannot afford it. Therefore, by allowing undocumented students to qualify for in-state tuition, universities are not losing money; rather, they are gaining money from students who would otherwise not have attended.

Irma Aboytes,
"Undocumented Students and Access to Higher Education,"
Journal of Gender, Race and Justice, *2009.*

ceive, than just, manifested towards us. What I ask for the negro is not benevolence, not pity, not sympathy, but simply justice. The American people have always been anxious to know what they shall do with us. . . . Do nothing with us! Your doing with us has already played the mischief with us. . . . All I ask is, give him a chance to stand on his own legs! Let him alone! . . . Your interference is doing him positive injury."

A quick check of the full Douglass speech reveals that the sentence immediately preceding Thomas' selective quote is as follows: "I look over this country at the present time, and I see Educational Societies, Sanitary Commissions, Freedmen's Associations, and the like,—all very good." Thus, Douglass opens the paragraph by praising a host of abolitionist affirmative action programs that provided the foundation for the Reconstruction era's Freedmen's Bureau, the most far-reaching affirmative action program ever instituted by the federal government.

Another significant sentence that Thomas edited out of Douglass' speech was one that would have clarified the context for "Do nothing with us!" That sentence was "Gen. Banks was distressed with solicitude as to what he should do with the Negro." (Note: Banks had instituted a notoriously discriminatory labor policy in Louisiana, claiming that it was necessary to help prepare blacks to handle freedom.)

Douglass expressed his concern with Banks' policy early in his address: "I hold that that policy is our chief danger at the present moment; that practically enslaves the Negro, and makes the [Emancipation] Proclamation of 1863 a mockery and delusion. . . . That I understand Gen. Banks to do—to determine for the so-called freedman, when, and where, and at what, and for how much he shall work, when he shall be punished, and by whom punished. It is absolute slavery. It defeats the beneficent intention of the Government, if it has beneficent intentions, in regards to the freedom of our people."

From his early Civil War experience recruiting black soldiers, Douglass knew he had good reason to question the sincerity of General Banks. In *Forged in Battle: The Civil War Alliance of Black Soldiers and White Officers*, Joseph T. Glatthaar writes: "Free black militia officers in New Orleans whom Maj. Gen. Benjamin Butler had accepted into federal service in September 1862 were rapidly weeded out for purposes of racial purity by his successor, Maj. Gen. N.P. Banks ... regardless of qualifications or competence.... Initially Banks tried to challenge these black officers on grounds of competence, which proved fruitless in many cases, particularly since they knew tactics and regulations as well as most white volunteer officers and had proven themselves very capable of command during combat."

'Let Him Alone!'

Perhaps the most outrageous deletion in Thomas' mangled quotation is the following sentence (in the original, it came immediately after "Let him alone!"). "If you see him on his way to school, let him alone, don't disturb him! If you see him going to the dinner table at a hotel, let him go! If you see him going to the ballot-box, let him alone, don't disturb him! If you see him going into a work-shop, just let him alone."

In a recent reaction to the Court's decision, Elaine R. Jones, president and director-counsel of the NAACP [National Association for the Advancement of Colored People] Legal Defense and Educational Fund, has declared incredulously that "the Court has the impression that the white students who are suing had higher scores than all the black students who got into Michigan. It is not true. Also, plenty of white students got in with lower scores." In 1860, Douglass captured the astigmatic, color-blind vision of the Supreme Court justices, observing that prejudice is "always blind to what it never wishes to see, and quick to perceive all it wishes."

During his tenure on the Supreme Court, Justice Thomas has acquired the image of a man meekly seeking the approval of his conservative brethren on the Court, while humbly enduring their patronizing treatment. He himself has admitted playing that demeaning role during his early attempts to join the conservative power structure. In a 1987 speech before the Heritage Foundation, Thomas lamented: "There was the appearance within the conservative ranks that blacks were to be tolerated but not necessarily welcomed. . . . There was the constant pressure and apparent expectation that even blacks who were . . . conservative publicly had to prove themselves daily. . . . Certainly, pluralism or different points of view on the merits of . . . issues was not encouraged or invited— especially from blacks. And, if advice was given, it was often ignored. . . . For blacks the litmus test was fairly clear. You must be against affirmative action and against welfare. And your opposition had to be adamant and constant or you would be suspected of being a closet liberal. . . . It often seemed that to be accepted within the conservative ranks and to be treated with some degree of acceptance, a black was required to become a caricature of sorts, providing sideshows of anti-black quips and attacks."

Justice Thomas' verbal caricature of Frederick Douglass in his *Grutter* dissent demonstrates that he is still willing to engage in these demeaning sideshows from the bench of the Supreme Court.

Periodical Bibliography

The following articles have been selected to supplement the diverse views presented in this chapter.

Lola Adesioye — "Saying Sorry for Slavery Isn't Enough," *The Guardian* (UK), July 31, 2008.

Zoe Aiano — "Racism and Reform: The Treatment of Immigrants and Other Minorities in Law Enforcement," *The New Presence: The Prague Journal of Central European Affairs*, Spring 2009.

Phil Boas — "An In-Depth Discussion with Senator Ron Gould, Foe of Guest-Worker Bill," *Arizona Republic*, May 18, 2008.

Camille Charles et al. — "Affirmative-Action Programs for Minority Students: Right in Theory, Wrong in Practice," *The Chronicle of Higher Education*, March 27, 2009.

Fernando Diaz — "Driving While Latino: Officers Are Pulling over Hispanic Drivers at a Disproportionately High Rate, and the Consequences Can Go Well Beyond a Ticket," *The Chicago Reporter*, March–April 2009.

Eric Johnson and Elizabeth Brandt — "Targeting Diversity: A Critical Account of Language Policy and Public Education," *Harvard Journal of Hispanic Policy*, 2009.

National Review Online — "Aloha Segregation," February 23, 2010.

Yuxiang Wang — "Language, Parents' Involvement, and Social Justice: The Fight for Maintaining Minority Home Language," *Multicultural Education*, Summer 2009.

**OPPOSING VIEWPOINTS® SERIES**

CHAPTER 4

What Does the Future Hold for Race Relations?

Chapter Preface

When Se Ri Pak joined the Ladies Professional Golf Association (LPGA) Tour in 1998, she was the only Korean golfer. Her skill and success turned her into a role model for other golfers; in 2010, 45 of the 129 international players on tour were from South Korea, representing nearly a fifth of all active tour players. (In fact, Korean television is the largest source of LPGA revenue.) So it caused no small amount of controversy in 2008 when, then LPGA commissioner, Carolyn Bivens announced to the Korean players—and not to players from any other country—that they would have to learn to speak communicable English or be put on suspension. Almost immediately, sponsors pulled their support from the LPGA and a California senator suggested that the LPGA could be banned from doing business in the state for violating anti-discrimination laws. Within a few weeks, the rule was rescinded, but not after causing much embarrassment for its leaders and players.

It is hard to argue that this rule had racist intentions. True, it came during a period of LPGA history when very few Americans were winning events, but the rule was more likely prompted by marketing concerns than hurt feelings and national pride. Winners who do not speak English rely on translators, and are not as easily transformed into a media-friendly personality that attracts an enthusiastic fan base and its money; Bivens thought she had the LPGA's best interest in mind. But because the LPGA board of directors was at the time composed entirely of Americans, they did not fully understand the implications of offending a fifth of their best players and their countrymen, and instead put the entire organization at risk. The globalization of sports and entertainment is a relatively new phenomenon that requires new ways of thinking about markets and is highly vulnerable to unrealized assumptions and misunderstandings about other people. The LPGA was still behaving as if it were an American group with a primarily American audience, and not realizing that the Korean players were bringing in a large audience of their own.

Fortunately for the LPGA, South Korea is still a strong supporter of women's golf and the incident did not cause irreparable damage to their relationship. As cross-cultural interactions increase in number, so will cross-cultural conflicts. How well people entering into interracial or cross-cultural relationships can excuse ignorance, accept responsibility, identify shared interests, and think creatively will influence how well they can solve problems or how large they make them.

The following chapter examines some of the ways that people of different races and cultures will relate to each other in the future, and explores whether they will be able to overcome their differences and build a joint identity or if they will fail to find any common ground and settle into patterns of polite or antagonistic estrangement.

> *"Generation Y, the O—as in, Obama—generation, millennials—whatever you want to call us . . . we have emerged as the most racially integrated demographic in our nation's history."*

Barack Obama Will Bring Black and White Americans Together

Keli Goff

Keli Goff, author of Party Crashing: How the Hip-Hop Generation Declared Political Independence, *emerged as a political pundit during the 2008 presidential election, and appeared as an expert on youth and minority voters on national news programs. The following viewpoint first appeared in the book* The Speech: Race and Barack Obama's "A More Perfect Union," *a collection of original writings about then-presidential candidate Barack Obama's speech in response to the racially inflammatory remarks made by Reverend Jeremiah Wright in Chicago in 2008. Goff optimistically interprets the speech as a definitive turning point toward racial integration in the United States.*

As you read, consider the following questions:

1. According to a *New York Times* article quoted in the viewpoint, how did young voters influence older voters during the Obama campaign?

2. What fundamental difference does the viewpoint author see between Dr. Martin Luther King Jr.'s "I Have a Dream" and Barack Obama's "A More Perfect Union" speeches?

3. According to cultural critic Michaela Angela Davis (quoted in the viewpoint), Obama's speech was a promise of what?

For many members of the post-civil rights generation, [Barack] Obama's mere existence is a powerful symbol of just how different their American experience is from their parents' and grandparents'. His multiracial makeup makes him in many ways the perfect political face for a generation that has become so defined by diversity that the growing popularity of racially ambiguous models in advertisements and actors in film was the subject of a 2004 *New York Times* article. Retailers were bending over backward to reach a generation of consumers whose worldview was increasingly defined as a rainbow. Hence the ubiquitous United Colors of Benetton ads that ran for years featuring fair-skinned, freckle-faced models sporting Afros next to almond-colored models with blond curls or Asian models with dreadlocks. While such ads might have caused some to ponder aloud, "Hmmm. I wonder what they are," for this generation the answer was obvious. They are American. That's what America looks like. And there's no reason the president shouldn't look like that.

As a testament to the increasingly fluid notions of race emerging among younger people, that same *New York Times* article described the U.S. Census Bureau as "stumped" by the number of Americans, nearly seven million, who checked more than one racial category in the 2000 census, the first time respondents were able to do so. The trend was particularly popular among younger Americans. Those under the age of eighteen were twice as likely as adults to identify themselves as multiracial, making members of Generation Y under the age of twenty-five the most racially diverse people in American history.

There are plenty of younger Americans who may not have grown up with Obama's braided heritage, yet have grown up poly-lingual and -cultural—that is, speaking and negotiating the multitude of language and cultural registers that those who float between worlds often do. For my young, black female friends and I, speaking the language of [television show] *Sex and the City*, with its Manolos, cosmos, and "He's just not that into you's," was just as essential as speaking the language of *Girlfriends*—*Sex and the City*'s browner and sometimes funnier counterpart. For some of my white friends, knowing the lyrics, of Dr. Dre's "Ain't Nuthin' but a 'G' Thang" was just as essential as knowing the lyrics of Nirvana's "Smells Like Teen Spirit." And for my friends of all races, growing up knowing and loving the Huxtable family of *The Cosby Show* was just as essential as knowing and loving your own. . . .

Race has been America's greatest obsession since the nation's inception. And yet, in the last two decades, something extraordinary has happened. After more than two centuries of de jure [legal] segregation, America has emerged as both a mosaic of cultures held together by its national identity and a melting pot, witnessed by the uptick in transracial/transcultural unions. The hip-hop generation, Generation Y, the O—as in, Obama—generation, millennials—whatever you want to call us, as the generations who have come of age after the civil rights movement in this country, we have emerged as the most racially integrated demographic in our nation's history. But more than that, we are the most socially and culturally integrated.

Children Lead Their Parents

In many ways, the cultural integration of this country has been more important than the legal one. A common sentiment once expressed by segregationists was that you could not legislate people's feelings. This is fundamentally true. The legal battles for equality were only part of winning the larger war (a very important part but a part nonetheless). Equality as we now know it was ultimately won not in the courtroom or even in the court of public opinion but in the court of cultural opinion, namely the defining cultural moments that have brought us together.

A *Vanity Fair* salute to the legendary music label Motown noted that when the [musical group] Temptations began performing in the South in the mid-sixties, a rope was placed within the audience to divide blacks from whites. Singer Smokey Robinson recounted receiving letters from young white fans who would say that they loved his music but kept it hidden from their parents, who would not approve. He then noted that only a few short years later he began receiving fan mail from whites that would say, "Our kids turned us on to your music." Around the same time, the rope once used to divide blacks from whites at Temptations concerts was removed.

If music broke down barriers within the baby boomer generation, then it blew them up altogether for the boomers' children and grandchildren. While Motown brought blacks and whites together on the same dance floors and in the same concert halls, hip-hop brought them together period. Even hip-hop's fiercest critics cannot deny that some of our nation's most defining moments of cultural integration have stemmed from hip-hop. When [rap group] Run-DMC joined [rock group] Aerosmith for a rock-meets-rap version of the Aerosmith classic "Walk This Way," the song, and, perhaps more important, the 1986 video, which ended up in nonstop rotation on MTV, sent a powerful message to both blacks and whites that they could not only enjoy the same music but also make beautiful music together—literally. In a nod to the cultural significance of the moment—which was not lost on the artists involved—the video features a wall between the two acts literally being knocked down. A few years later, hip-hop would produce one of its and America's brightest stars. Will Smith introduced America to a different face of hip-hop, one that not only white and black kids but their parents could appreciate (even if those same parents just didn't "understand"). But eventually Smith would go on to become culturally significant beyond the confines of hip-hop. He has emerged as the most bankable film star in Hollywood. This means that a rapper turned actor is now the celebrity with whom a majority of Americans—black, brown, Asian, Native American, and white, young and old—would most like to spend their evening at the movies.

We have come a long way since Motown.

Much as their parents convinced their own parents to give the [musical group] Supremes and the Temptations a chance, the generation who grew up with "Walk This Way" and *The Fresh Prince of Bel-Air* [Will Smith's television show] have in many ways nudged their own parents a step further, introducing them not only to their favorite black artists but to their own black friends. The post-civil rights generation has served as a powerful bridge for racial reconciliation in this country, and by extension as a powerful bridge for Barack Obama's candidacy.

As the *New York Times* article "Young Obama Backers Twist Parents' Arms" noted, "Young supporters of Mr. Obama, who has captured a majority of under-30 primary voters, seem to be leading in the pestering sweepstakes. They send their parents the latest Obama YouTube videos, blog exhortations and 'Tell Your Mama/Vote for Obama!' bumper stickers." The article revealed that Senator Bob Casey of Pennsylvania had decided to endorse Obama largely on the strength of the enthusiasm displayed by his teen daughters for Obama's candidacy.

Casey's endorsement was particularly noteworthy because he had initially planned to stay neutral in the race. Additionally, Casey, who is white and Catholic, represented constituencies that Obama had struggled with: Catholics and working-class white voters in Pennsylvania. . . .

A "Post-Race" Society

It is only natural that historians, pundits, and others would strive to compare [Obama's] "A More Perfect Union" [speech] to that other landmark speech on race, Dr. Martin Luther King Jr.'s "I Have a Dream." Subject matter aside, however, the speeches are markedly different, shaped by the different experiences of the men who gave them and the vastly different circumstances under which they were compelled to give them. While Dr. King was trying to convince Americans of different colors not to fear one another, Obama was ultimately trying to convince Americans to trust one another and, in their capacity, to perfect the union. Though they may sound similar, these are in fact two very different goals. The greatest difference between the two men's speeches lies in the audiences to which they delivered them. King found himself speaking to an audience primarily populated by generations bracketed by 1896's *Plessy v. Ferguson* and 1954's *Brown v. Board of Education* [Supreme Court cases]. For many of these Americans, little had really changed in their day-to-day lives.

Obama spoke to a very different audience, one populated by some Americans who could still recall the America that King had dreamed of bringing *change* to all those years before, but increasingly by more Americans who were living the dream—as was Obama himself. While King's speech represented a lofty dream for many, Obama's "A More Perfect Union" represented reality for many more—particularly younger Americans.

Obama issued a disclaimer regarding just what he believed "A More Perfect Union" could ultimately accomplish: "Contrary to the claims of some of my critics, black and white, I have never been so naive as to believe that we can get beyond our racial divisions in a single election cycle, or with a single candidacy—particularly a candidacy as imperfect as my own." Clearly he sold himself and the speech short. The speech's greatest legacy is that by talking frankly and openly about race, it finally allowed our nation to begin to move forward in a way we had been unable to before. Journalist and cultural critic Michaela Angela Davis noted in the aftermath of "A More Perfect Union," "By not ignoring the issue of race, I felt many folks like me could actually start to let it go. You can only forgive if you promise never to forget. His speech was a promise that we didn't need to fully identify ourselves and our work by race and racism, nor did we have to turn our backs on it and live in denial." She continued, "Though I identify myself as a post-civil rights, hip-hop generation, 'Barack generation' woman, I am not [of the] post-race generation. This speech helped lighten the burden of full identity by race and started giving us permission to begin being, just simply being."

When I asked my incredibly optimistic and full-of-life eighty-seven-year-old grandmother if she had ever thought that she would see a black president elected in her lifetime, she responded that she hadn't given the matter much thought over the years, but fundamentally, "no." She didn't have it down on her list of things she would get to see in her long, extraordinary life. And yet, she—a woman who had endured a life that had included segregation, the Great Depression, and hard, backbreaking work in the cotton fields—lived long enough to see America become a country in which her granddaughter *could* grow up believing that the election of a black president was not only a possible dream but a viable reality. And in some ways this says more about the evolution of our nation than Obama's actual election to the presidency does. However, it is Barack Obama's ability to successfully bridge the gap between vastly different American experiences with his message of hope, forgiveness, and, most of all, letting go and looking forward that makes "A More Perfect Union" such an important contribution to the American conversation.

And it gives me hope that one day my young niece will also grow up and live in a continuously evolving and *changed* America, one where she will read this essay that ponders the issue of race and politics and find herself asking, "What was all the fuss about?"

"After classes—and after the occasional Obama rally—most black and white students on college campuses go their separate ways."

Barack Obama Will Not Make Black and White Americans Closer

Jonathan Kaufman

Jonathan Kaufman is a Pulitzer Prize winning reporter who currently works as the education editor for Bloomberg News; prior to this position he worked for fifteen years at the Wall Street Journal. *He is also the author of two books and a frequent lecturer at major universities. The following viewpoint describes black and white student relations at Duke University, a North Carolina school with black students forming about ten percent of the student body. Although black and white college students readily worked together on Barack Obama's presidential campaign, Kaufman reports that this camaraderie did not translate into significant friendships in their personal lives.*

As you read, consider the following questions:

1. Why does student Jazmyn Singleton say that only two-thirds of the black students on campus can be described as "black"?

2. What differences in the definition of "friendship" did Eduardo Bonillo-Silva find between black and white students?

3. According to the author, why do many black students report that they choose to room with other black students at Duke University?

Walking into his "Race and Politics" class recently, David Sparks, a white Duke University political science graduate student, considered whether to move from his usual seat in the group of white students who always clustered at one end of the seminar table to sit with the black students who typically sat at the other end.

Mr. Sparks didn't do it. "It would have felt too conspicuous," he says. Still, on Tuesday's primary here [May 13, 2008], Mr. Sparks plans to vote for Sen. Barack Obama for president. That's an easier choice, he says.

"When you're actually trying to change your behavior, you are putting more on the line compared to voting in the privacy of the booth," he says. "There are millions and millions of people voting for Obama. In no way are you sticking your neck out."

Across the country, college campuses have become hotbeds of support for Sen. Obama. Nationally, 70% of Democrats ages 18 to 24 favor Sen. Obama compared with 30% for Hillary Clinton, according to a recent poll by Harvard's Institute of Politics. Many black and many white students wear their Obama buttons and "Got Hope?" T-shirts proudly as a sign that they are part of a post-Civil-Rights generation more welcoming of change and diversity than their parents.

But after classes—and after the occasional Obama rally—most black and white students on college campuses go their separate ways, living in separate dormitories, joining separate fraternities and sororities and attending separate parties.

"It's much harder to be a white person and go to an all-black party at Duke than vote for Obama," says Jessie Weingartner, a Duke junior. "On a personal level it is harder to break those barriers down."

Jazmyn Singleton, a black Duke senior agrees. After living in a predominantly white dorm freshman year, she lives with five African-American women in an all-black dormitory. "Both communities tend to be very judgmental," says Ms. Singleton, ruefully. "There is pressure to be black. The black community can be harsh. People will say there are 600 blacks on campus but only two-thirds are 'black' because you can't count blacks who hang out with white people."

The racial divisions among college students are striking both because of the fervor for Obama and the increasing diversity on campus. Colleges offer a unique opportunity for students to get to know each other in a relaxed atmosphere where many of the issues that often divide blacks and whites, like income and educational levels, are minimized amid the common goals of going to class, playing sports and going to parties.

About 10% of Duke students are African-American, compared to 4.5% two decades ago; they include many popular athletes as well as student leaders. The newly elected head of the graduate and professional student association is an African-American woman. Black and white students live together in the same group of dorms during freshman year, though they can join fraternities and sororities and select their roommates starting in sophomore year.

Like many colleges, Duke sponsors initiatives to address race relations on campus, an effort that gained added impetus following the widely publicized incident two years ago [2006]

Shared Religion, Separate Lives

"I think [our school] has a lunch-table problem," Baylor [University in Waco, Texas] English professor Tom Hanks tells me frankly. "For the most part, black students stay with blacks, Asians stay with Asians, and WASPs [White Anglo-Saxon Protestants] stay with WASPs." He adds, "This doesn't surprise me but it troubles me." In this sentiment, Hanks is hardly alone: Self-segregation at religious colleges concerns many students and faculty, but few can explain it. And just as at secular colleges, there is a sense of hopelessness in combating it.

Is it a lost cause? In part, yes. There is certainly an extent to which religious colleges cannot overcome the racialized social environment in which they exist. Secular society's attitudes about race are bound to permeate the walls of these schools. While for the last few decades, that has been undoubtedly positive ... the politically correct attitude that race should be the defining characteristic of a person, influencing every aspect of their character, is one that religious colleges could probably do without. But the schools' own acknowledgment that members of a particular ethnic group are best suited to bring its other members into the fold supports secular society's tacit message that only people of the same race can truly understand each other.

Naomi Schaefer Riley, God on the Quad, *2005.*

when white lacrosse players hired a black stripper to perform at a party and the woman then falsely accused several of the students of raping her.

The Obama campaign has created another opportunity for blacks and whites on campuses to interact. At the University of North Carolina in nearby Chapel Hill, "seeing someone wearing an Obama pin is a reason for a connection," says Tessa Bialek, a white junior. "It's a reason to wave to someone on the way to class."

"When I am working on the Obama campaign I really don't see a person's race," says Kandis Wood, an African-American senior at Duke.

But working or voting for an African-American running for president doesn't necessarily bridge differences—on campus or, later, in the workplace. Following a recent discussion in one of his classes about the campaign, in which most students expressed support for Sen. Obama, Eduardo Bonilla-Silva, a Duke sociologist, asked his white students how many had a black friend on campus. All the white students raised their hands.

He then asked the black students how many of them had a white friend on campus. None of them raised their hands.

The more he probed, Mr. Bonilla-Silva says, the more he realized that the definition of friendship was different. The white students considered a black a "friend" if they played basketball with him or shared a class. "It was more of an acquaintance," recalls Mr. Bonilla-Silva.

Black students, by contrast, defined a friend as someone they would invite to their home for dinner. By that measure, none of the students had friends from the opposite race. Mr. Bonilla-Silva says when white college students were asked in a series of 1998 surveys about the five people with whom they interacted most on a daily basis, about 68% said none of them were black. When asked if they had invited a black person to lunch or dinner recently, about 68% said "no." He says his own research and more recent studies show similar results.

Ben Bergmann, a white freshman and head of the Duke Democrats who has been volunteering for the Obama campaign and traveled to South Carolina to canvass voters, says he enjoys the campaign "because a lot of different people come together and there is a real sense of togetherness. There is no awkwardness between blacks and whites."

On campus, however, social barriers remain, Mr. Bergmann says. "There is a black guy in my dorm and we hang out—there is a core group of like 30 people and we will all hang out on a Friday night. But I don't think we would hang out one-on-one. I don't think he would call me up or I would call him up."

Some white students at Duke and other schools blame racial division on the fraternity and sorority system, which breaks down along racial lines, and the presence of "themed" housing which allows black students to live together.

Some blacks respond that black students—like all students—room with people they are comfortable with. What's more, they say living among blacks eases some of the pressure and isolation of being a minority at a predominantly white institution.

"When I was at Williams [College in Williamstown, Mass.] I thought I had a lot of white friends," says Ashley Brown, a black graduate student at Duke. "But I look on Facebook and I see that they all go to visit each other. But none of them come down here to visit me." She pauses. "Of course, I haven't gone to see them either."

This semester, Max Entman, a white Duke senior who is voting for Sen. Obama, took a class called "Cultural Polities and Soul Music" taught by one of Duke's most popular African-American professors. Unlike most Duke classes, this class was predominantly African-American. "It was the most racially evocative experience I have had at Duke," he says. "It's the one place where I had the most interaction with black students, talking about racial issues, racism, black identity, black culture."

Looking back, Mr. Entman says he regrets one thing. As part of the class, students had to attend five concerts of soul music outside of class.

He went to the concerts with his white roommate.

> "You can't integrate large numbers of Muslims in a country that has a cultural base that is Christian."

Muslims Cannot Be Integrated into Western Culture

Christopher Caldwell

Christopher Caldwell is a columnist for the Financial Times, *a contributing writer for the* New York Times Magazine, *and a senior editor at the* Weekly Standard. *The following viewpoint is excerpted from his book,* Reflections on the Revolution in Europe: Immigration, Islam, and the West. *Caldwell describes the conflicts that arise between the current generation of Muslim immigrants and the Westernized people who expect them to adapt to their cultures. Caldwell argues that these modern Muslim immigrants do not assimilate as well as immigrants do from other countries—or even as well as Muslim immigrants did in the past.*

As you read, consider the following questions:

1. According to the viewpoint author, what percentage of Germans believe that Muslims "want to remain distinct"?

2. In what way do younger generations of Muslim immigrants to France identify themselves differently than older generations do, according to the author?

3. How, according to the viewpoint, is television preventing European Muslim immigrants from assimilating into the cultures of their new homes?

Whenever Europeans worried about the long-term assimilability of immigrants, it was Muslims they worried about most. Sometimes it was Muslims they worried about exclusively. In Denmark, where the right-wing Danish People's Party (DF) had frightened the ruling coalition into passing Europe's strictest laws against immigration, the DF leadership was at pains to convey that it did not consider *all* immigrants problematic. "They are no problem—totally integrated," said the priest and DF parliamentarian Jesper Langballe of the many Tamils who had settled in his own parish in Jutland. "The problem is, you can't integrate large numbers of Muslims in a country that has a cultural base that is Christian." Rikke Hvilshøj, the country's integration minister at the time, said that this was not an unusual view. Denmark had received large immigrant flows from Hungary in 1956 and Poland in 1968, not to mention an unusually big contingent of Vietnamese boat people in the late 1970s and early 1980s. "When Danes speak of immigrants today," she said, "it is not Hungarians or Vietnamese they are talking about."

The view of the European man-in-the-street (of 88 percent of Germans, for instance) was that Muslims "want to remain distinct"—but nowhere was that opinion reflected in government policy. The official view was that Muslims were much the same as any other immigrant group, and while Muslims had admittedly shown a reluctance to embrace European culture thus far, inexorable historical processes were at work. Over the long term, Muslims could no more constitute a culture apart than immigrants in previous centuries had, according to political leaders, and the reason was Muslim diversity. Not only is Islam a varied spectrum of beliefs and cultures—Arab and non-Arab, Sunni and Shia, traditional and modern—but that spectrum is further refracted by Islam's sudden entry into Europe. In what sense do English-speaking Pakistanis share a culture with Italian-speaking Moroccans or German-speaking Turks? To speak of "the Muslims" was an ignorant stereotype, an optical illusion. It was what the French would call an *amalgame* [amalgam].

Certainly diversity among Muslims is greater than it looks. Neighborhoods that outsiders perceive as "Pakistani" may be Pakistani and Bengali, and the Pakistanis in it may be divided between people who think of themselves as Punjabis and others who are Mirpuris. A single Parisian neighborhood made up of Algerians who emigrated in the 1960s (Ménilmontant, for example) might be divided between Arabs and Berbers. A Rhineland neighborhood made up of Turks who arrived in the 1960s (Marxloh, for instance) will almost certainly be split between religious Sunnis and Alevites, as well as between ethnic Turks and Kurds. Knowledgeable about this diversity, many Muslims' grow impatient with being lumped together as an undifferentiated mass. "What do you mean, 'Islam'?" one German social worker asked a journalist at *Der Stern* [news magazine]. "There's no such thing as single, unique Islam." The French sociologist Dounia Bouzar wrote a book called *"Mister Islam" Doesn't Exist*. But for all its pleasing glibness, this harping on diversity is misguided. It is like saying that, because a Volvo is different from a Volkswagen, there's no such thing as a car. While diversity certainly exists among Muslim groups, its importance has been overstated.

European or Muslim First?

There is a reason that diversity became such a treasured myth among well-meaning Europeans: A utopia could be built on it. If Islam can exist in so many forms, they asked, why not a

European form, which would graft onto the religion not just a loyalty to Muslims' new countries of citizenship but also a respect for constitutional rights known to be anathema [detested or shunned] in almost every part of the Muslim world? The late French scholar of Islam Jacques Berque first raised the idea of replacing Islam *in* France with an Islam *of* France in the late 1980s, and since then the idea, along with the catchphrase, has become popular among bureaucrats and intellectuals throughout Europe. Stefano Allievi, probably the leading Italian sociologist of Islam, wrote of younger generations in which "Islam in Italy is becoming Italian Islam." Creating a "German Islam" out of a bunch of German Muslims is the explicit goal of the Islamkonferenz launched by interior minister Wolfgang Schäuble in 2006.

What has actually happened in most countries in Europe is the opposite—a partial embrace of the national identity of the new country has been followed by a withdrawal to the religious identity of the old. This shift is more pronounced among younger generations. In Berque's own France, the country that has devoted the most resources to domesticating Islam, young people of Muslim descent think of themselves as Muslim before they think of themselves as French. Asked what element characterizes them best, about a third of Muslim students answered that it was their religion, versus fewer than 5 percent of native French children who said the same. The leftist journalist Alain Gresh notes that the expression "second generation" was never used for previous generations of young French people whose parents happened to be Italian and Polish. This could be a failure of the French traditions of *citoyenneté* [citizenship]—it is more likely a sign that, however strong those traditions may be, the attachment of this generation to its ancestral traditions is stronger.

The situation is similar in Britain. In early 2007, the think tank Policy Exchange released a troubling study. It found that nearly a third (31 percent) of British Muslims thought they

European Muslims and Anti-Semitic Outbreaks

The majority of anti-Semitic attacks in Europe since 9/11 [2001] have been perpetrated by members of the very same Muslim communities now claiming to be Europe's "new" Jews. In almost every case of harassment and violence documented by CIDI [Center for Information and Documentation on Israel] in Amsterdam, the victims reported that their persecutors were of North African Muslim origin. It is Muslim gangs who have been responsible for many of the anti-Jewish hate crimes across the rest of the continent as well. In mid-2006, for example, in the heavily Muslim area of southwest Berlin, a group of young local women assaulted a twenty-six-year-old female student, a dual citizen of Israel and Germany, because they heard her speaking Hebrew on her cell phone.

By the end of last year [2006], following the summer's conflict between [Lebanese organization] Hizballah and Israel, Muslim offenses against Jews in Europe had reached unprecedented heights.

Efraim Karsh and Rory Miller,
"Europe's Persecuted Muslims?" Commentary, 2007.

had more in common with Muslims in other countries than with their fellow citizens. Only half referred to Britain as "my country." The sense of belonging to Britain was *higher* among those over 45 (55 percent) than among those 18 to 24 (45 percent). Military enlistment offers another clue to how "British" young British Muslims feel. In February 2007, British authorities uncovered a plot hatched by local Muslims in Birmingham to kidnap a British Muslim soldier and torture him to death on a video to be disseminated over the Internet. It emerged that the targeted soldier was one of only 330 Muslims in the British armed forces, a number that not even dogged recruiting efforts have sufficed to raise. Britain's Muslims were joining the military at roughly one-twentieth the rate of other Britons.

In theory, Germany has a better chance of forming the kind of national Islam that European governments claim to want, not because of any particular wisdom in its policies but because of the orientation of the Turkish culture out of which most of its immigrants came. "People look with pride on their own history of modernization since [President] Atatürk," wrote the journalist Jörg Lau, "and see themselves, for the most part, as already part of Europe and the West." This is not an indication that Turks are more willing to adapt to Germany than other immigrant groups are to their respective new countries, only that they have less need to adapt.

One way to get a sense of German Turks' deepest allegiances is to look at their choices about burial. All Muslim organizations in Germany have burial funds (*Bestattungsfonds*) to which community members subscribe. Muslim burial has generally meant burial in the subscriber's country of origin. According to a study by the Center for Turkey Studies in 2000, only 5 percent of Turks could see themselves being buried in Germany. The fact that 68 percent favor the establishment of Muslim cemeteries in Europe—which would allow burial in shrouds rather than coffins, among other adjustments—may be an optimistic sign. But it indicates that the price of a more "European" Islam will be a more Islamic Europe. When asked whether there is "a special, German form of Islam," 68 percent of German Turks say there is not. They are evenly split on the question of whether the laws of Islam are even compatible with the rules of German society—52 percent say they are, while 46 percent say they are not. . . .

Diverse Muslims or One Islamic People?

Conditions are ripe for the various Muslim communities of Europe to coalesce in a unified identity. The United States offers the best example of how, in an age of mass immigration, sub-identities get melded into larger ones. "Hispanic" identity was largely a fictional category when federal census takers invented it in the 1970s. "Hispanic" was a linguistic, not a sociological, term. It was useful as a proxy for northbound immigration flows, but there was no such thing as a "Hispanic" person. Spanish speakers themselves complained that the "Hispanic" category did not respect the difference between, say, a white Cuban pianist and an Indian cowboy from Mexico. But affirmative action and Spanish-language marketing and television combined to turn this abstract identity into a real one. Today there really is such a thing as a Hispanic (or Latino) identity, made up of Chilean-Americans and Mexican-Americans competing for the same bilingual marketing jobs at corporations in New York, of Puerto Ricans and Bolivians watching the same shows on Univisión, and of new migrants working in industries—such as landscaping and restaurants—where Spanish is a lingua franca [language of the people].

In Europe, formerly distinct communities' interests have started to converge into a larger Muslim culture. In most immigrant housing projects, satellite dishes run up the buildings like buttons, picking up the news from home. This would seem to throw into reverse television's historic role as an engine of immigrant assimilation, keeping open lines of communication from the old country. But in other ways, television does indeed assimilate immigrants. It is just that it assimilates them into something other than traditional European culture. It assimilates them into globalized Islam. The Muslim scholar Yusuf Qaradawi's weekly fatwa [legal opinion] show on al-Jazeera [Arabic-language network], for instance, is watched all over Europe.

Just because Europe is a main audience of this new, online Islamic culture does not mean that culture will be pro-European. It may mean the opposite. Muslim websites are no less marked by slapdash verification and an incendiary political idiom than their counterparts in the non-Muslim world. One of the paradoxes of the Internet is that this most modern of media has brought new power to premodern habits of discourse: rumor, gossip, urban myths, old wives' tales. A lot of young Palestinians in Denmark, most of them refugees from the civil war in Lebanon, believe the welfare payments they accept in Denmark put them in no position of indebtedness toward the Danish state, because the money has been effectively stolen from families like their own. "They say, 'The money comes from the United Nations,'" recalls one integration expert in Copenhagen. "'They send it to Denmark, and Denmark takes half. That's why I'll never be loyal to the Danes.'" More than half (56 percent) of British Muslims do not believe Arabs committed the atrocities of September 11, 2001, versus 17 percent who do.

European Muslims often wind up locked in the ancient and present-day grievances of their homelands—and other people's homelands. Extremists who recruit volunteers for jihad [holy war] abroad have often done so by using videos, with stirring musical accompaniment, that show Muslims mistreated, humiliated, wounded, and killed in various trouble spots; one friend of the four 7/7 suicide bombers [who attacked the London Underground subway on July 7, 2005] told the *Wall Street Journal*, "They were aware that we Muslims are suffering the most in the world, be it Iraq, Afghanistan or Palestine."

That Muslims suffer the most is the focal point of an increasing number of European Muslims' identity. The day after the unspeakable violence in the London Underground in July 2005, Imran Waheed of the radical group Hizb ut-Tahrir insisted, "We have far greater experience as victims of terror than as perpetrators of terror." Who is the "we" that he is referring to here? It is not, by any stretch of the imagination, Britons. He added that the British Muslim community's reaction to Britain's participation in wars in Afghanistan and the Middle East had until then been "remarkably restrained."

"More than six-in-10 U.S. Muslims (63%) say they see no conflict between being a devout Muslim and living in a modern society."

Muslims Can Develop an American Identity

Pew Research Center

The Pew Research Center is a nonpartisan organization that provides information on the issues, attitudes, and trends shaping America and the world. The following viewpoint is excerpted from Muslim Americans, *a joint project of the Pew Research Center for the People and the Press and the Pew Forum on Religion and Public Life. A survey of more than 60,000 Muslims living in America, ranging from recent immigrants to native-born converts, reveals that their attitudes toward American culture, religious practice, political and social values, and extremism are by and large in line with mainstream American beliefs and practices.*

As you read, consider the following questions:

1. According to the Pew Research Center, what percentage of U.S. Muslims identify themselves as American first?

2. What percentage, according to the viewpoint, of U.S. Muslims say new Muslim immigrants should "mostly adopt American customs and ways of life"?

3. According to the survey, how do views on interfaith marriage differ between Muslim men and women?

While Muslim Americans are somewhat less upbeat about their life and circumstances than are other Americans, the differences are modest, and Muslims in the United States are mostly satisfied with their communities and their lives. As with the general public, however, Muslims are less satisfied with the overall direction of the country.

On the question of assimilation, a plurality of U.S. Muslims (43%) say that Muslim immigrants arriving in the U.S. should mostly adopt American customs and ways of life, though a significant minority (26%) thinks that new immigrants should try to remain distinct. Nearly half of Muslims say they think of themselves as a Muslim "first," while 28% say they think of themselves as an American "first." However, Muslims in Western Europe and in predominantly Muslim countries are generally much more likely to think of themselves primarily as Muslims, rather than as citizens of their countries.

Happiness and Community

Nearly eight in 10 U.S. Muslims say they are rather "very happy" (24%) or "pretty happy" (54%) with their lives. This is modestly lower than the proportion of the general public expressing this view (36% very happy and 51% pretty happy).

Few notable demographic differences emerge in overall levels of personal satisfaction. Muslim immigrants are somewhat less content (74% very or pretty happy) than Muslims who were born in the United States (84%). Bigger differences emerge among younger and older Muslims: Just one in 10 Muslims younger than 30 say they are not too happy with

Muslims Coming to America Today Should ...

Question: Which comes closer to your view? Muslims coming to the US today should mostly adopt American customs and ways of life, OR Muslims coming to the US today should mostly try to remain distinct from the larger American society.

	Adopt American Customs %	Remain Distinct from U.S. Society %	Both* %	Neither/ [Don't Know]* %
All U.S. Muslims	43	26	16	15
Men	48	26	15	11
Women	38	26	18	18
18–29	43	39	13	5
30–39	41	24	18	17
40–54	49	22	16	13
55+	41	17	17	25
Religious Commitment				
High	37	37	18	8
Medium	39	26	18	17
Low	58	17	12	13
Native-Born	37	38	11	14
African American	31	47	9	13
Other Races	44	27	15	14
Foreign-Born	47	21	18	14
Arrived Pre-1990	55	15	15	15
1990 or Later	43	25	19	13

*Based on volunteered responses

TAKEN FROM: Pew Research Center, "Survey of American Muslims," 2007.

their lives, while 89% are very or pretty happy. Among Muslims ages 30 and older, 21% are unhappy with how things are in their lives, while 74% say they are very or pretty happy. A similar age-related difference is evident in the general public.

Like other Americans, Muslims are generally pleased with the communities in which they live. More than seven in 10 rate their community as an "excellent" (28%) or "good" (44%) place to live. In the general population, 41% rate their communities as excellent, and 41% as good. Three in four Muslim immigrants (76%), compared with 65% of all native-born Muslims, rate their home communities as either "excellent" or "good" places to live.

Contentment with their lives and communities does not extend to their views about the country. Most Muslim Americans (54%) say they are dissatisfied with the overall direction of the county—a critical view shared by an even larger proportion of the general public (61%).

Hard Work Pays Off

If anything, Muslim Americans are more likely than the general public to believe that hard work is the path to success: 71% of Muslim Americans say that "most people who want to get ahead can make it if they work hard." A somewhat smaller percentage of the general public (64%) agrees with this statement.

Notably, African American Muslims are less convinced than other U.S. Muslims—both native-born and immigrants that hard work brings success. Fewer than six in 10 African American Muslims (56%) agree with this principle, compared with 75% of other native-born Muslims, and 74% of all foreign-born Muslims.

The views of African American Muslims about whether hard work leads to success are on par with those of African Americans more generally. When the same question was asked last year [2006] in a nationwide Pew survey, 59% of African Americans agreed that hard work brought success.

U.S. Muslims: Americans First?

Asked whether they think of themselves first as an American or first as a Muslim, a 47% plurality of U.S. Muslims say they consider themselves Muslims first; 28% say they think of themselves first as Americans. In May 2006, when U.S. Christians were asked a parallel question, 42% said they think of themselves as Christians first, while 48% said they are Americans first.

The survey findings suggest the question is as much a measure of personal religious commitment as an expression of patriotism to the United States. Among Muslim Americans who have a high level of religious commitment, 70% say they consider themselves to be Muslims first. But among those with low religious commitment, just 28% see themselves this way, while a 47% plurality identifies first as American, and 12% say they consider themselves equally Muslim and American.

The link between religiosity and self-identity is similar among Christians in America. By roughly two to one (59% vs. 30%), U.S. Christians who say religion is very important identify as Christians first, while those who say religion is less important identify as Americans first, by a margin of 76% to 18%. Similarly, most white evangelical Protestants (62%) say they primarily identify themselves as Christians rather than Americans, while most white mainline Protestants (65%) identify as Americans first.

The relationship between religious attendance and religious identity may partially explain why younger Muslims are more likely to consider themselves as Muslim first. By a margin of more than two to one (60% vs. 25%), most Muslim Americans under age 30 say they think of themselves as Muslims first. About half of all Muslims under age 30 say they attend mosque at least once a week compared with slightly more than a third of Muslims age 30 and older. Among young people who attend weekly, nearly seven in 10 (68%) say they identify first as Muslim compared with 36% of all Muslims who seldom or never attend services.

Muslim Identity and Extremism

The poll finds that one's identification as Muslim or American also relates to opinions about Muslim extremism. For example, 13% of those who think of themselves primarily as Muslims believe that suicide bombing to defend Islam from its enemies can be often or sometimes justified, compared with 4% of those who say they are American first. Still, overwhelming majorities of both groups reject suicide bombing as a strategy, including 85% of those who identify primarily as Americans and 79% who consider themselves Muslims first.

Somewhat larger differences emerge when it comes to views about who carried out the 9/11 [2001] terrorist attacks on the World Trade Center and the Pentagon. Those who identify themselves first as Muslim are twice as likely (40% vs. 20%) to say these attacks were not carried out by groups of Arabs. Slightly fewer than three in 10 U.S. Muslims (28%) who think of themselves primarily as Muslim say they believe the 9/11 attacks were carried out by groups of Arabs while six in 10 Muslims (61%) who think of themselves first as American say Arabs were responsible.

Assimilation vs. Maintaining Identity

Like other U.S. religious groups, Muslims believe that their religious convictions can fit comfortably in a world of rapid change and shifting values. More than six-in-10 U.S. Muslims (63%) say they see no conflict between being a devout Muslim and living in a modern society, a belief they share with many Muslims around the world.

Still, Muslim Americans struggle to find a balance between two worlds and two very different cultures. They divide over the best strategy for Muslim immigrants to pursue when they arrive in the United States. The largest share (43%) say new arrivals should "mostly adopt American customs and ways of life." But 26% believe Muslims should "mostly try to remain distinct from the larger American society." Another 16% volunteer that new immigrants should try to do both.

Muslims who were born in the United States—particularly African American Muslims—are more likely than Muslim immigrants to argue against new arrivals assimilating fully into American life. Nearly half of African American Muslims (47%) say that Muslim newcomers to the U.S. should strive to keep their religious and cultural identities; just 31% believe they should try to assimilate. By contrast, pluralities of other native-born Muslims and foreign-born Muslims say that Muslims arriving in the U.S. should try to adopt American customs.

Gender and religiosity also are linked to views about whether new Muslim immigrants should assimilate. Men are more likely than women to say Muslims should adapt (48% vs. 38%). Devout Muslims are less inclined to favor new arrivals integrating into American life. Among those Muslims with the strongest religious commitment, fewer than four in 10 (37%) say immigrants should adopt American customs, a view held by more than half (58%) of less religious Muslims.

In general, Muslim Americans reject the idea that their fellow Muslims in the U.S. are becoming less religious. Roughly four in 10 (43%) say that Muslims in the United States are not changing very much in terms of their religiosity. If anything, a greater percentage says that U.S. Muslims are becoming more religious (31%) rather than less religious (17%). Two-thirds of those who say that Muslims in the United States are becoming more religious say that is a good thing, while about half of those who say Muslims are becoming less religious view this as a bad thing.

Other questions portray U.S. Muslims as a community in the process of assimilating with the larger society. Nearly half (47%) report that all or most of their close friends are Muslims, while 51% report having relatively few Muslims in their inner friendship circle. Muslim American women are particularly likely to have mostly Muslim friends. A majority of Muslim women (56%) say that all or most of their close friends are Muslims, compared with 39% of Muslim men.

For the most part, Muslim Americans say it is acceptable for a Muslim to marry a non-Muslim, even though Islamic law prohibits a Muslim woman—but not a man—from marrying outside the faith. Overall, 62% believe it is "okay" for a Muslim to marry a non-Muslim, while 24% say it is unacceptable; 11% volunteered that it depends. More than eight in 10 (84%) Muslim Americans with a relatively low level of religious commitment say there is nothing significantly wrong with interfaith marriages, compared with just 45% of highly religious U.S. Muslims. In addition, many more men (70%) than women (54%) think it is okay to marry a non-Muslim.

"*The European-American experience demonstrates unambiguously that ... relationships will spring up among individuals from different groups as contexts like neighborhoods become more diverse.*"

Members of Different Races Can Become More Integrated in the Future

Richard Alba

Richard Alba is Distinguished Professor of Sociology at the Graduate Center of the City University of New York. The following viewpoint is excerpted from his book, Blurring the Color Line: The New Chance for a More Integrated America. *Alba argues that the divisions between members of different racial groups will narrow as economic and educational opportunities open up to current political and religious outsiders, and as changing population demographics encourage interracial marriages.*

He offers three strategies to promote and accelerate these social changes: narrowing the education gap, increasing class mobility, and encouraging social proximity to the dominant (white) culture.

As you read, consider the following questions:

1. According to the author, in what ways are Asian Americans viewed as permanent foreigners?

2. Why does the author argue that mixed race children of today will be better equipped to navigate white cultures than mixed race children of previous generations?

3. What group of people has the privileged position in the labor market, according to the author?

The changes in the social position of Asian Americans illustrate compellingly that racial visibility is not an insurmountable barrier to increasing social intimacy between the members of a minority and the majority. Although Asians were once subject to vicious forms of racism—in the second half of the nineteenth century, the Chinese on the West Coast were frequently driven out of their homes and businesses by whites and even lynched—today they are increasingly integrated in largely white social milieus. They frequently share residential environments with many whites: analysis of 2000 Census data revealed that the average Asian American resided in a neighborhood where whites were the majority and Asians formed less than a fifth of the population. Neither Hispanics nor blacks typically resided in neighborhoods where they were outnumbered by the white majority. The high rate of intermarriage by young U.S.-born Asian Americans shows that they are also entering into white families.

These changes do not mean a complete ending of racist slights and attacks for Asians. Yet even here one can envision that these expressions of racism will be forced to cede further ground as the integration of Asians, still very fresh in historical terms, continues. One complaint of many Asian Americans is that they continue to be viewed by many other Americans as permanent foreigners: in encounters with strangers, they experience being interrogated on where they "really come from" or complimented on how well they speak English, even when they have been born in the United States and have grown up with English as their mother tongue. Such questions and comments are a form of bias, a prejudgment based on skin color that obscures individual realities. However, these slights, as deplorable as they are, must still be placed in the contemporary context: since Asians represent a small portion of the U.S. population (5 percent in 2006) and Asian adults still are largely foreign born at this point in our history (outnumbering the U.S. born by more than 3 to 1 as of 2006), most other Americans have little or no experience with the U.S.-born generations of Asian Americans. In the not-too-distant future, the Asian population will increase and the proportion of it born in the United States will, too, and many more whites will be able to recognize the diversity among Asian Americans. The integration of Asians into mainstream communities will speed this process.

Interracial Families Become More Common

Also changing the character of relations of minorities with whites will be the growing population of individuals with mixed ancestry. The mixed ancestry engendered by racial intermarriage today is fundamentally different from that in the past, which occurred in the context of the profoundly unequal relations that existed between racial minorities and whites. Thus the racially mixed ancestry found by DNA analysis among African Americans because of past sexual encounters between whites and blacks was mostly produced outside of marriage and not recognized by whites, who as a group held overwhelming power to determine the social place of minority individuals and defined that of mixed-race persons according to the "one drop" [of African blood] rule. Because of it, Thomas Jefferson's white descendants were able to refuse for the better part of two centuries to recognize, even informally, his descendants from his children with the slave Sally Hemings. Many African-American families did retain memories, and frequently bitter ones, of white ancestors, as [African American activist] Malcolm X's memoir attests. But racial intermarriage is today an increasingly common occurrence and now involves 4–5 percent of married whites, with the precise figure depending on whether mixed-race partners are counted as whites or minorities. Most of this intermarriage takes place with Asian or Hispanic partners; intermarriage by whites with African Americans is less common, though it is increasing. Intermarriage, even at such a modest level, has a surprisingly widespread impact on whites' family circles: using a smaller estimate of intermarriage than is found in recent data, the demographer Joshua Goldstein has estimated that one in seven whites possesses a close-kin network that includes at least one non-white. The children of racial intermarriages are by and large not being raised within minority ghettoes, as were the mixed-race children of a century ago, but with access to the family circles of their white and minority parents. This access does not predetermine how they will identify and be identified as adults—those are issues that demand research attention—but whatever that outcome, such individuals are likely to feel comfortable in their social relations with whites as well as with same-minority individuals. They are individuals who have the potential to blur racial boundaries because of their dual-sided membership.

Moreover, the intermarriage rate of whites with minorities is likely to continue to increase. This prediction is supported by the well-known relationship of marriage patterns to population composition: *ceteris paribus* ["all other things being equal"], as the population proportion of potential partners with a given characteristic increases, so does the frequency of marriage with them. The rising percentage of minorities among the young adults of the future is beyond doubt; and unless whites and/or minorities become markedly less willing to marry across boundaries, the percentage of whites marrying nonwhites is destined to rise. This is especially the case for marriages of whites to Asians and Hispanics, the populations that will be expanding most rapidly. (Paradoxically, the same composition principle also leads to the conclusion that the rates of Asians and Hispanics who marry within their ethnic group will increase, as may already be happening. There is no inherent contradiction here because of the changing composition of the population, which involves a decline in the relative number of whites.) There will also almost certainly be a rise in the number of marriages between whites and mixed-race persons, both because of the growing proportion of the latter and because of their unusually high propensity to marry whites. In sum, the proportion of the population who have close family ties in multiple racial groups and who thus blur the boundaries between them seems certain to increase in the future (whether or not these individuals see themselves as part of a mixed-race population and report themselves in this way on the Census). . . .

Suggested Policies for Change

The opportunity to alter the ethno-racial boundaries of American society through increasing diversity at its middle and upper levels, achieved by the mobility into these tiers of native minorities and the second generation of contemporary immigrant groups, in the end, is just that: an opportunity, not a predictable outcome. This leads to the obvious next question: What can be done to help bring boundary change about? . . . It is hard to avoid the sense that this may be an especially propitious moment to raise this question because the [Barack] Obama administration, just installed, is bringing new sensitivities and priorities to Washington [D.C.], for example,

Integrated Schools Develop Social Unity

The current emphasis on academic outcomes, or test scores, leads citizens and educators alike to ask whether racial integration is necessary—must students be sitting next to ethnically and racially different students in order to learn? The answer to that question depends on the purpose of public education. Research examining the effect of segregation on test scores is mixed. However, if public education encompasses larger goals, such as developing a civil society and social capital, then indeed, the peer environment in public schools should be a major consideration of education policy. . . .

Analysis found that individuals from communities with more highly segregated school districts reported the lowest level of social trust. Furthermore, the findings suggest a relationship between individual social capital measures and interracial friendships. For example, respondents who are more likely to socialize informally, participate in organized community activism, and trust others, are also more likely to have interracial friendships. Also, individuals who report themselves as more politically conservative are less likely to have interracial friendships. . . .

If one of the key purposes of public education is to prepare youth for successful participation in civil society, which involves much more than test scores, then the issue of diversity in our public schools needs to be addressed.

Hinckley A. Jones-Sanpei, "Public School Segregation and Social Capital," Journal of Gender, Race and Justice, *2009.*

ranking job creation and improvements in education among its most important goals. The analysis of a prior episode of change, in particular the mass assimilation of the white ethnics in the middle of the twentieth century, suggests some points of leverage on the processes involved.... Public policies will be needed to:

1. Narrow the educational gap between white and minority Americans.

The greatest threat to future boundary change lies in the lagging educational attainments of U.S.-born black and Hispanic Americans compared with non-Hispanic whites and Asians. The gap does not loom so large when all forms of postsecondary education are considered, and this fact suggests that minorities are prepared to take advantage in large numbers of opportunities in the middle of the labor force, in those jobs in the second and third quartiles where some degree of postsecondary training will be an advantage or a requirement. However, the gap is quite substantial, on the order of 2 to 1, when it comes to college and university credentials at the baccalaureate level or higher. In addition, U.S.-born Hispanics have substantially higher dropout rates from high school than do white Americans.

The educational gap can be narrowed, if not closed, but it will require national will to do so. The United States has done this before. The educational lag of the children of southern and eastern European immigrants from rural backgrounds, such as the southern Italians, was of the same order of magnitude, yet within a few decades, between 1940 and 1970, the second and third generations of these groups caught up to, even surpassed, white American educational norms....

2. Open channels of mobility wider.

The evidence we have seen throughout indicates indisputably that minorities continue to be disadvantaged in the labor market, even when they have postsecondary education. A variety of research perspectives—for example, studies of managers—converge in finding the privileged position of white males in the labor market. U.S.-born blacks and Hispanics achieve a lower occupational placement than do native-born whites with similar levels of education, and they earn less than do whites in the same occupations. While to some degree these ethno-racial inequalities could be explained by differences in the quality of the educational institutions attended by whites versus minorities, it is highly improbable that all of them can. A reasonable conclusion is that minorities continue to face discrimination in the labor market.

That being the case, policies of affirmative action are going to continue to be needed during the coming quarter century, which will afford a remarkable opportunity to erode the ethno-racial divisions that have dominated U.S. society for so long. Affirmative action can be narrow in its scope—ensuring, for example, merely that the pool of individuals under consideration for a position is not homogeneous in ethno-racial terms—but undoubtedly more broad-gauge forms of it are going to be required to make large strides in the direction of ethno-racial parity. This means, in other words, that minorities are going to have to be given some degree of preference when they are as qualified as whites. Even if the evidence for discrimination is viewed by some as questionable, there is still a strong rationale for affirmative action in the upper tiers of the labor market. . . .

3. Help minorities convert improved socioeconomic position into social proximity to whites.

In addition to vertical, socioeconomic mobility, the diminishment of ethno-racial boundaries requires horizontal intergroup relationships of trust and intimacy that perforate boundaries and take the air out of the social distinctions at their core. Mobility for minorities without an increase in equal-status, minority-majority relationships leaves boundaries in place; and since the majority remains ultimately the more powerful group, the socioeconomic gains of the minority are vulnerable. This is true even if the white majority eventually becomes a numerical minority in the United States, as population projections suggest may happen by mid-century (however, as forecasts, the population projections are suspect because they assume ethno-racial categories will have the same meaning in the future as they do today). Research on African Americans continues to reveal the difficulties that successful parents face in passing on their socioeconomic advantages to their children, who in a racially divided society are at greater risk of sliding downward than are comparable white children. Cross-boundary relationships between individuals of unequal status likewise do not diminish boundaries (and perhaps enhance them by validating the stereotypes that are encrusted in their social walls). Such relationships were common enough in the Jim Crow [segregation laws of the] South, for example, where they generally conformed to the social conventions of master-servant relationships.

Social policy obviously cannot force individuals into relationships of friendship and trust. What it can legitimately do, however, is provide access to social contexts where resources are concentrated and where, in the absence of integration, advantages such as high-quality schooling for children are monopolized by dominant social groups. Residential neighborhoods exemplify such contexts. Although the effects of increasing diversity within American communities are currently a matter of debate, the European-American experience demonstrates unambiguously that, given the right conditions, relationships will spring up among individuals from different groups as contexts like neighborhoods become more diverse in their composition. A belief in the moral equality of minority newcomers, similar to that which accompanied the white-ethnic social ascent in the mid-twentieth century, will help to facilitate such linkages.

> *"American communities have grown more racially, politically, and economically homogenous in recent decades. . . . When the subject is community diversity, Americans talk one way but behave another."*

America's Democratic Future in a Post-racial Age

Rich Benjamin

Rich Benjamin is a senior fellow at Demos, a New York City nonpartisan think tank that advocates for and advises policy makers on a more equitable economy with widely shared prosperity and opportunity, and a vibrant and inclusive democracy with high levels of civic engagement. The following viewpoint is excerpted from his book, Searching for Whitopia, *an account of his two-year journey through the towns and neighborhoods of white America, or "Whitopia." The white population of these perceived utopias grows each year, and Benjamin predicts a future in which these racially segregated enclaves continue to attract residents, particularly young families and senior citizens.*

As you read, consider the following questions:

1. According to the author, what are the defining characteristics of a Whitopian town?

2. What are three qualities the author asserts are associated with white neighborhoods?

3. Into what three categories does the viewpoint author place the American towns that comprise Whitopia?

Imagine moving to a place where you can leave your front door unlocked as you run your errands, where the community enjoys a winning ratio of playgrounds to potholes, where you can turn your kids loose at 3 p.m., not to worry, then see them in time for supper, where the neighbors greet those children by name, where your trouble-free high school feels like a de facto private school, where if you decide to play hooky from work, you can drive just twenty minutes and put your sailboat on the water, where the outdoor serenity is shattered only by each seagull's cry, where you can joyride your off-road vehicles (Snowmobiles! ATVs! Mountain bikes! Rock crawlers!) on Nature's bold terrain, where your family and abundant friends feel close to the soil, and where suburban blight has yet to spoil your vistas. Just imagine.

If you could move to such a place, would you?

If so, you would join a growing number of white Americans homesteading in a constellation of small towns and so-called "exurbs" that are extremely white. They are creating communal pods that cannily preserve a white-bread world, a throwback to an imagined past with "authentic" 1950s values and the nifty suburban amenities available today.

Call these places White Meccas. Or White Wonderlands. Or Caucasian Arcadias. Or Blanched Bunker Communities. Or White Archipelagos. I call them Whitopia.

A prediction that made headlines across the United States ten years ago is fast becoming a reality: By 2042, whites will no longer be the American majority. A related, less-reported trend is that as immigrant populations—overwhelmingly people of color—increase in cities and suburbs, more and more whites are living in small cities and exurbs.

Failures of Multiculturalism

"So many of the people that are here have come from areas where they have seen diversity done badly," says Carol Sapp, a prominent civic and business leader in St. George, Utah, a bona fide Whitopia.

Christine Blum moved to St. George in 2004 after living for twenty-four years in Los Angeles. "When I lived in California, everyone was a liberal, pretty much," recalls Christine, the president of the local women's Republican group. "I wanted to be around people who shared my political views." She groans remembering the conversations in California where liberals bashed the GOP [Republican party] and the social settings in which she felt censored. "It's like, I don't want to say what I really think, 'cause they're going to think I'm an evil, right-wing fascist." In California, she worked in the animation field, mostly for Disney, and as an assistant director on *King of the Hill* [an animated television show]. She came to St. George to escape the big city and to start a new career as a cartoonist and illustrator.

Christine says she doesn't miss the many hues in L.A.'s population: "For me it's just the restaurants."

Denise Larsen moved to the St. George area from Milwaukee [Wisc.] with her husband and young daughters in 1997. "When we heard the gang shootings, we thought 'It's time to move,'" Denise tells me over soda pop at Wendy's. "This kid tried to leave a gang; they shot up his dad down the block from us. I guess you don't try and leave a gang. We could no longer let our kids ride their bikes around. Here, they could ride all the way down to the Virgin River, and we don't have to worry about it." For a mother frustrated with having her daughters bused across town due to a desegregation order, fed up with shoveling snow, and terrified of the gunshots ringing out, her new, Whitopian community is the perfect elixir. . . .

The Attractions of Whitopia

What exactly is a Whitopia? A Whitopia (pronounced why • *toh* • pee • uh) is whiter than the nation, its respective region, and its state. It has posted at least 6 percent population growth since 2000. The majority of that growth (often upward of 90 percent) is from white migrants. And a Whitopia has a *je ne sais quoi* [an indefinable quality]—an ineffable social charisma, a pleasant look and feel.

Bill Frey, a senior fellow at the Brookings Institution, a prestigious nonpartisan think tank based in Washington, D.C., has been documenting white population loss from ethnically diverse "melting pot suburbs" for decades. And that loss is significant. During the 1990s, the suburbs of greater Los Angeles lost 381,000 whites, and other California suburbs, such as Oakland and Riverside-San Bernardino, and also the Bergen-Passaic suburbs in New Jersey, lost more than 70,000 whites each. The rate of white population loss from the melting pot suburbs of Honolulu, Los Angeles, San Francisco, Miami, and several other major suburban areas *exceeded* the rate of out-migration from their central cities.

"The Ozzies and Harriets [after a television show of the 1950s] of the 1990s are bypassing the suburbs or big cities in favor of more livable, homogenous small towns and rural areas," Frey presciently forecast in 1994, when this phenomenon was nowhere near its maturity.

To be sure, race and immigration are not the only factors pushing whites from cities and "melting pot suburbs." Whites, like Americans of all races, have felt pushed by stagnant job opportunities, pricey housing markets, congestion and traffic, crumbling public facilities and services, and neighborhoods that seem hostile to raising children. Quality-of-life and pocketbook factors matter greatly.

Matthew Dowd, a founder of Vianovo, a blue-chip management and communications consulting firm with clients worldwide, who also served as chief strategist for Bush-Cheney '04 [presidential campaign], explained to me in a telephone interview that Americans don't trust the unfolding economy, regardless of who is in the White House. "Unemployment numbers, inflation rates, and all those figures don't really tell the story anymore, because people have lost some faith in all the major institutions of the country—from churches, to political parties, to the government—and so they have this great deal of anxiety about what they can count on." Dowd believes this anxiety has bred a longing for strong communities, though he doesn't get into the racial traits of those communities. "Part of what's happened in our society over the last twenty years," he adds, "is that people have lost their connection to each other and to the community organizations that they or their parents or their grandparents participated in. So they're looking for this sort of new community."

This type of "new community" is really back-to-the-basics, placing as it does a premium on sporting, volunteerism, neighbors, friends, faith, family, and hearth. People inhabiting this "new community" are bonded by a common investment and vision. This vision matters as much as economics—Whitopia has grown briskly during past recessions *and* throughout the economic roar of the late 1990s.

"I wish I could go back in time," says Lynn Jensen, a middle-class mother in Livingston County, Michigan, a Whitopian exurb. "We had stable lives. Mom could stay at home, and we could afford it. Life was slower. God, I'm sounding like my parents—all nostalgic for the old days. But it's true: There wasn't trouble then like there is today."

"The California I grew up in was a little paradise," says Phyllis Sears, an eighty-three-year-old resident of St. George,

Utah. Other St. George residents compare the dry mecca to the Southern California of decades past.

What Draws People to Whitopia

The high tide of Whitopian migration typically crests at two pivotal moments in the life cycle: when residents start raising children and when they retire. Children and senior citizens face very different challenges, but both age groups are more vulnerable than young and middle-aged adults. Children and seniors particularly require physical and emotional security in their homes and communities. Hostages to the dictates of time—the demands of the future and the spells of the past—parents carve idealized lives for their kids, just as the elderly guard idealized memories, perhaps eager to leave their particular legacy. Thinking seriously about childhood, one's children's or one's own, whisks a potent undercurrent of nostalgia into Whitopian dreaming.

Whitopian migration results from tempting *pulls* as much as alarming *pushes*. The places luring so many white Americans are revealing. The five towns posting the largest white growth rates between 2000 and 2004—St. George, Utah; Coeur d'Alene, Idaho; Bend, Oregon; Prescott, Arizona; and Greeley, Colorado—were already overwhelmingly white. Certainly whiter than the places that new arrivals left behind and whiter than the country in general. We know why white folks are *pushed* from big cites and their inner-ring suburbs. The Whitopian *pull* includes economic opportunity, more house for your dollar, a yearning for the countryside, and a nostalgic charm. . . .

Most whites are not drawn to a place explicitly because it teems with other white people. Rather, the place's very whiteness implies other perceived qualities. Americans associate a homogenous white neighborhood with higher property values, friendliness, orderliness, hospitability, cleanliness, safety, and comfort. These seemingly race-neutral qualities are subconsciously inseparable from race and class in many whites' minds. Race is often used as a proxy for those neighborhood traits. And, if a neighborhood is known to have those traits, many whites presume—without giving it a thought—that the neighborhood will be majority white.

As much as creative elites in Manhattan and Hollywood might like to dismiss this trend as "corn-fed racism," or to ridicule it as "boringly bourgeois," it *is* our present and future. Sorry, city sophisticates. Between 1990 and 2000, America's suburban periphery grew by 17 million people. By contrast, city cores grew by a fraction—only 3 million people. In the years since, outer suburban and exurban counties have grown at triple the rate of urban counties. For all the noise over gentrification, skyscrapers, and metrosexuals, the real action is happening on the periphery: remarkable white migration, resilient economies, and significant political power. . . .

"Americans Say They Like Diverse Communities—Election, Census Trends Suggest Otherwise," declares the title of a 2009 study released by the prestigious Pew Research Center. "Despite most respondents' stated preference for 'diversity,'" the study concludes, "American communities have grown more racially, politically, and economically homogenous in recent decades, according to the analyses of 2008 election returns and U.S. Census data. When the subject is community diversity, Americans talk one way but behave another."

When those pop-up lists beckon you from your Web browser ("Retire in Style: Fifteen Hotspots!"), or those snappy guidebooks flirt with you from the bookstore shelves (*America's 25 Best Places to Live!*), ever notice how white they are?

Think of Whitopia in three ways—as small towns, boomtowns, and dream towns. Some Whitopias are fiber-optic Mayberries [fictional town from the *Andy Griffith Show*], small towns and counties that take pride in their ordinariness. Other Whitopias are boomtowns, entrepreneurial hotbeds that lure a steady stream of businesses, knowledge workers, and families.

In the low-tax, incentive-rich boomtowns, the costs of living and doing business are cheaper than in the big-shot cities (even during the present recession). Finally, there are dream towns, Whitopias whose shimmery lakes, lush forests and parks, top-notch ski resorts, demanding golf courses, and deluxe real estate trigger flights of ecstasy, luring the upscale whites who just love their natural and man-made amenities.

In short, the lure of Whitopia includes affordable mortgages and old-time values for modest-income families (small towns), economic prospects for blue-collar and high-income professionals (boomtowns), and luxuriant recreation and choice homes for the privileged (dream towns).

Cell phones, BlackBerrys, laptops, networked file servers, point-'n'-click travel booking, e-mail, and the Internet make physical offices more obsolete and permit much of the skilled workforce to telecommute. And though Americans grow increasingly enamored of virtual offices, they are just as enamored of real communities. Geography matters less than it once did in the workplace, but more in Americans' personal lives. The digital revolution has intensified people's ambivalence over physical offices precisely as our attachment to our homes and natural surroundings is becoming more dear. As such, Whitopia flourishes as a constellation of small towns, boomtowns, and dream towns made possible by the digital revolution, and made "necessary" by long-standing social and cultural anxiety.

Periodical Bibliography

The following articles have been selected to supplement the diverse views presented in this chapter.

Zoe Burkholder — "The Future of Racially Integrated Schools," *Education Week*, May 26, 2010.

Sam Cacas — "Black-Asian Unity: Why We Need to Talk about Race Relations Beyond Individual Incidents," *AsianWeek*, April 27, 2010.

Gerald Early — "The End of Race as We Know It," *Chronicle of Higher Education*, October 10, 2008.

Joshua Hoyt — "'We Are America': Immigrants and Social Capital in the United States Today," *National Civic Review*, Spring 2009.

Joel Kotkin — "A Race of Races: The U.S.' Emergence as the First Multiracial Superpower," *Forbes*, February 2, 2010.

Latoya Peterson — "The Forgotten Promise of Obama's Race Speech," *The American Prospect*, January 18, 2010.

Shannon Proudfoot — "Mixed-Race Families Swelling in Canada, StatsCan Says," *Montreal Gazette*, April 21, 2010.

Rebecca Roberts — "The 'Post-Racial' Conversation, One Year In," *Talk of the Nation* (NPR), January 18, 2010.

Sam Roberts — "No Longer Majority Black, Harlem Is in Transition," *New York Times*, January 5, 2010.

Gregory Rodriguez — "Tackling Race, One Beer at a Time," *Los Angeles Times*, August 3, 2009.

Hope Yen — "Interracial Marriage Is Still Rising, But Not as Fast," *Associated Press*, May 26, 2010.

For Further Discussion

Chapter 1

1. Biologists and geneticists are hesitant to describe "race" as a physical characteristic, and will readily argue the viewpoint that race does not exist. Sociologists and other researchers insist that race exists in society, so it is a real phenomenon. How does searching for a biological origin of race affect dialogues about race relations? Would the discovery of genetic racial differences be of political or social benefit or harm?

2. Po Bronson and Ashley Merryman argue that awareness of racial differences is innate and that children need to be taught how to understand and manage them in order to participate in a multicultural society. Luigi Castelli and his coauthors show how easily children can be taught to view racial differences in a negative way. Should children be taught about race? Would children need this instruction if society already enjoyed racial equality?

Chapter 2

1. Christina Thompson claims that socioeconomic barriers are more difficult to overcome than racial barriers in interpersonal relationships, but Derek A. Kreager found that high school students are relatively intolerant of interracial romances. Because students often attend schools in their neighborhood or private schools that reflect their parents' values, they have fewer socioeconomic barriers to overcome. What differences in adulthood and adolescence might contribute to opinions toward racial differences in romantic partnerships?

2. Free trade theorists say that all people in a society benefit when goods and services are produced as cheaply as possible. From this point of view, even African Americans who lose their jobs to Latino immigrants willing to work for less money enjoy the lower prices and greater availability that cheap labor enables. What balance should a government strike between protecting the employment of groups of people and providing the most affordable economy to all the people within its borders?

Chapter 3

1. If racial profiling is affecting how fairly laws are enforced, who is responsible for this problem? If police officers are unaware of their racial biases, should they be blamed? Is the prevalence of racial profiling an unfortunate coincidence, a social necessity, a matter of training police officers, or a matter of better screening applicants to the police force in the first place? What might be other ways to eliminate this problem?

2. Even proponents of affirmative action programs reiterate that they are temporary measures intended to narrow racial achievement gaps and not give certain groups of people privileged status over others. What would be some social or economic indicators that affirmative action programs are no longer needed? What kinds of evidence would demonstrate that the goals of affirmative action had been achieved?

Chapter 4

1. The election of Barack Obama is heralded as the United States taking its first step toward a post-racial society in which race is utterly irrelevant. What does that mean to politicians and academics? What does that mean to ordinary people? Is it reasonable to expect that race will

someday in fact become irrelevant? Are there advantages to maintaining a society with distinct racial groups?

2. Is making predictions about the likelihood of voluntary racial segregation in the future a practical exercise? Do past examples of forced and voluntary racial integration and current population trends provide any basis for surmising how people might behave in the coming decades? Explain your answer using examples from the viewpoints in this chapter.

Organizations to Contact

American Civil Liberties Union (ACLU)
125 Broad St., 18th Floor, New York, NY   10004-2400
(212) 549-2500
e-mail: infoaclu@aclu.org
Web site: www.aclu.org

The ACLU is a nonprofit organization that provides legal assistance in court cases about civil liberties—often by filing lawsuits—and that acts as a legislative lobbying group to defend and protect civil rights. Issues identified by the ACLU as needing constant vigilance and attention range from racial justice and immigrant rights, to prisoners' rights, and the consequences of national security efforts.

Anti-Defamation League (ADL)
(202) 452-8310 • fax: (202) 296-2371
Web site: www.adl.org

The ADL was founded in 1913 to fight anti-Semitism but has since become an important organization that fights bigotry of all forms. In the United States it serves as a source of information about anti-Semitism, bigotry, and racism, monitors and exposes extremist groups, provides educational outreach to combat hate, and promotes cooperation among members of different religious faiths; it also conducts international programs to support its mission globally. It runs youth leadership programs to help people become active and informed in their communities and sponsors the Law Enforcement Agency Resource Network to help in the fight against extremism and terrorism.

Council for Responsible Genetics (CRG)
5 Upland Rd., Suite 3, Cambridge, MA   02140
(617) 868-0870 • fax: (617) 491-5344

e-mail: crg@gene-watch.org
Web site: www.councilforresponsiblegenetics.org

The CRG was founded by a coalition of scientists, public health activists, and reproductive rights activists to share with a general audience issues in the new fields of genetic technology. It publishes the magazine, *Gene Watch*, which monitors the social and ethical consequences of biotechnology, from genetically engineered foods to genetic privacy and discrimination. The central principles of the CRG are that the public must understand technological innovations and their implications, that the public must have a voice concerning the implementation of new genetic technology, and that social problems rooted in poverty and racism cannot be remedied by technology alone.

MAVIN Foundation

1425 Broadway, #517, Seattle, WA   98122-3854
(206) 622-7101
e-mail: info@mavinfoundation.org
Web site: www.mavinfoundation.org

The MAVIN Foundation's mission is to help build healthier communities by exploring the experience of mixed heritage people, transracial adoptees, interracial relationships, and multiracial families. MAVIN publishes the magazine *MAVIN*, and hosts the Mixed Heritage Center Web site, a national clearinghouse of information related to mixed heritage issues. MAVIN's *Multiracial Child Resource Book* is a handbook for parents and other people who serve multiracial children to help raise them with compassion and competence. The group also organizes social events at the local level and runs an online book club.

National Association for the Advancement of Colored People (NAACP)

4805 Mt. Hope Dr., Baltimore, MD   21215
(877) 622-2798
Web site: www.naacp.org

The NAACP was founded in 1909 in response to violence directed at black Americans; it played a large role in the Civil Rights movement of the mid-twentieth century. Its current mission is to ensure the political, educational, social, and economic equality of rights of all people and to eliminate racial hatred and discrimination. Its members encourage change through democratic processes and seek the enactment and enforcement of federal, state, and local laws securing civil rights. The organization has special offices for youth involvement, legal action, and advocacy and research for education, criminal justice, and health needs.

National Council on U.S.-Arab Relations
1730 M St. NW, Suite 503, Washington, DC   20036
(202) 293-6466 • fax: (202) 293-7770
Web site: www.ncusar.org

The National Council on U.S.-Arab Relations is a nonprofit, non-governmental, educational organization dedicated to improving American knowledge and understanding of the Arab world. It promotes programs for leadership development, people-to-people exchanges, lectures, publications, an annual Arab-U.S. policy makers conference, and the participation of American students and faculty in Arab world study experiences. The council also serves as an information clearinghouse and publishes newsletters, produces videos and live programs, and hosts podcasts.

Teaching Tolerance
Southern Poverty Law Center, Montgomery, AL   36104
(334) 956-8200
Web site: www.tolerance.org

Teaching Tolerance is a project of the Southern Poverty Law Center, a civil rights organization dedicated to fighting hate and bigotry. Its Web site is a resource for educators and other school professionals that includes classroom activities and ideas for professional development, as well as a catalog of resources that support tolerance curricula. The organization also produces videos, publishes the magazine *Teaching Tolerance* (free to educators), and sponsors the annual "Mix It Up at Lunch" day. Participating schools plan activities to encourage students to interact with peers outside of their established social circles, which are often divided by race or ethnicity.

United Nations Educational, Scientific, and Cultural Organization (UNESCO)

7, place de Fontenoy, Paris 07 SP   75352
    France
+33 (0)1 45 68 10 00 • fax: +33 (0)1 45 67 16 90
Web site: www.unesco.org

UNESCO contributes to the global fight against racism and discrimination through research and local educational programs and projects. With the United Nations Commissioner for Human Rights, UNESCO promotes tolerance, teaches adults and children how to become active participants in the transformation of their societies, and establishes a network of cities to share strategies for fighting racism, discrimination, xenophobia, and exclusion. Results of research studies performed by these cities are available on the UNESCO Web site.

U.S. Pan Asian American Chamber of Commerce Education Foundation (USPAACC)

1329 18th St. NW, Washington, DC   20036
(202) 296-5221 • fax: (202) 296-5225
e-mail: info@uspaacc.com
Web site: www.uspaacc.com

The USPAACC is a national, nonprofit organization that represents all Asian American groups in business, science, the arts, sports, education, and public and community services. It promotes successful partnerships and business growth in the marketplace, sponsors scholarships and internships to train future leaders, and uses the social and political influence of Asian Americans to promote economic growth through legislative advocacy and national trade associations.

Bibliography of Books

Geneive Abdo — *Mecca and Main Street: Muslim Life in America after 9/11.* New York: Oxford University Press, 2007.

Moustafa Bayoumi — *How Does It Feel to Be a Problem?: Being Young and Arab in America.* New York: Penguin Press, 2008.

Stephanie Rose Bird — *Light, Bright, and Damned Near White: Biracial and Triracial Culture in the United States.* Westport, CT: Praeger, 2009.

Adrian Burgos — *Playing America's Game: Baseball, Latinos, and the Color Line.* Berkeley, CA: University of California Press, 2007.

Arlene Davila — *Latino Spin: Public Image and the Whitewashing of Race.* New York: New York University Press, 2008.

Michael Dyson — *Come Hell or High Water: Hurricane Katrina and the Color of Disaster.* New York: Basic Civitas, 2007.

Korie Edwards — *The Elusive Dream: The Power of Race in Interracial Churches.* New York: Oxford University Press, 2008.

William McKee Evans — *Open Wound: The Long View of Race in America.* Urbana, IL: University of Illinois Press, 2009.

Karyn Folan — *Don't Bring Home a White Boy and Other Notions That Keep Black Women from Dating Out.* New York: Gallery Books, 2010.

Andrew Garrod and Robert Kilkenny, eds. — *Balancing Two Worlds: Asian American College Students Tell Their Life Stories.* Ithaca, NY: Cornell University Press, 2007.

Mark Gevisser — *A Legacy of Liberation: Thabo Mbeki and the Future of the South African Dream.* New York: Palgrave Macmillan, 2009.

Laura Gomez — *Manifest Destinies: The Making of the Mexican American Race.* New York: New York University Press, 2007.

Charles Henry — *Long Overdue: The Politics of Racial Reparations.* New York: New York University Press, 2007.

Fred Ho and Bill Mullen, eds. — *Afro Asia: Revolutionary Politics and Cultural Connections Between African Americans and Asian Americans.* Durham, NC: Duke University Press, 2008.

Noel Ignatiev — *How the Irish Became White.* New York: Routledge, 2009.

John Jackson — *Racial Paranoia: The Unintended Consequences of Political Correctness.* New York: Civitas Books, 2008.

Huping Ling, ed.   *Asian America: Forming New Communities, Expanding Boundaries.* New Brunswick, NJ: Rutgers University Press, 2009.

Meizhu Lui et al.   *The Color of Wealth.* New York: New Press, 2006.

David Pollock and Ruth Van Reken   *Third Culture Kids: Growing Up Among Worlds* (Revised Ed.). Boston: Nicholas Brealey Publishing, 2009.

Terrence Roberts   *Simple, Not Easy: Reflections on Community, Social Responsibility and Tolerance.* Little Rock, AR: Parkhurst Brothers, Inc., 2010.

Robert Rubinstein   *Peacekeeping Under Fire: Culture and Intervention.* Boulder, CO: Paradigm Publishers, 2008.

Beryl Satter   *Family Properties: Race, Real Estate, and the Exploitation of Black Urban America.* New York: Metropolitan Books, 2009.

Chilton Williamson, ed.   *Immigration and the American Future.* Rockford, IL: Chronicles Press, 2007.

Tim Wise   *Between Barack and a Hard Place: Racism and White Denial in the Age of Obama.* San Francisco: City Lights Books, 2009.

Leonard Zeskind   *Blood and Politics: The History of the White Nationalist Movement from the Margins to the Mainstream.* New York: Farrar Straus Giroux, 2009.

Index